"Brilliant and inspiring...a develop an Emotional Wellth mindset and skillset."

– Sam Horn, Founder & CEO The Intrigue Agency, author of 10 best-selling books, including *Talking On Eggshells: What to Say When You Don't Know What to Say*

"I have had the benefit of getting to know JC as a business executive, a competitive cyclist and great friend, and have appreciated the self-kindness mindset he demonstrates in everything he does. We are fortunate that he was able to capture and share this philosophy in his holistic Emotional Wellth Framework and shows us through examples how this can drive positive results in sports, business and personal relationships."

– Mike Wien, 4-time World Champion triathlete, college professor, retired marketing executive and author of *The Specific Edge: How Sustained Effort Wins in Business and Life*

"Antidote" is an inspiring story about the power of perseverance and positivity. It's also a provocative framework for success and all-around wellbeing. JC's story is sure to speak to anyone who's striving to make more of their life — and it's a refreshing reminder to enjoy the ride along the way.

– Mary Long, Podcast Host and Producer

"In the banking world we need refreshing thinking about how to prepare for retirement whether it is now or later. In *Antidote*, JC shares his easy-to-read A,B,C's of Money that can put you on the right track...today."

— Ramon Looby, President & CEO
Maryland Bankers Association

"In *Antidote*, we uncover the profound truth that life is a series of choices—and it's through these choices that we shape our resilience and growth. Life brings challenges, but how we respond; that's where the magic lies and how we move through them is what defines us.

By embracing the dynamic interplay of choice and movement, this book empowers readers to transform obstacles into opportunities for strength and clarity. Rooted in the wisdom of aligned living, *Antidote* provides the tools to navigate life's twists and turns with grace, cultivating emotional freedom and a foundation for a vibrant, abundant future."

— Teri Cochrane, CEO & Founder
Global Sustainable Health Institute,
precision wellness expert,
Best-selling author *Wildatarian Cookbook*

ANTIDOTE

A New
Emotional Wellth
Framework™
to Build Resilience

JC CHAMBERLAIN SR.

Antidote: A New Emotional Wellth Framework™ to Build Resilience

© Copyright 2024 John Chamberlain, Sr.

AntidoteThe**Book**.com

ISBN: 978-1629672908
Library of Congress Control Number: 2024924074

Interior Layout: Brian Schwartz
Cover Design: Tatiana Villa

r24-1212

Table of Contents

I AM THIRD.

The Emotional Wellth Framework

My Story - Show Up, Get Up, Rethink

As I look back on my life, I see physical and mental challenges that I've either overcome or learned from, even when I thought I couldn't. These stories fill this book. The specifics in my life, as an avid cyclist and businessperson, are probably quite different from the specifics of your life story.

In the end, it's how you *see* your story that matters most.

Bigger than my stories is the thread of meaning and opportunity that runs through them. It is my dearest hope that what I ultimately learned, every step and misstep of the way, can be seen as a system for dealing with life's challenges.

To that end, I have coined the word **"wellth,"** as the perfect union of abundance and healthy attitudes toward ourselves and other people.

How to apply it to your life? At the end of each chapter, you'll find a summary of lessons learned, discussion ideas and specific checkboxes to help you extract what points might be pertinent to you.

While I sincerely hope you do find these stories engaging, it is my bigger wish that my conclusions might inspire and encourage anyone dealing with dark times and deep questions to move through these and have an optimal outcome in your life.

The expansive sky was cloudless, with only phone lines piercing the clear blue. I was training to cover the most distance on a bicycle in one hour, a competition called the Hour Record. Every weekend, I would drive from Virginia to Ohio to visit my girlfriend, where I had discovered some inviting two-lane roads west of town that stretched across picturesque farms toward Plain City.

Up ahead, I noticed three cyclists and felt my heart beat faster with a surge of competitiveness. I increased my speed to catch them. I rode in a bigger gear while maintaining the same cadence for eight phone poles, and then eased back into a lower gear. After a half-hour of riding at my redline, I had made little progress. Just as I thought I couldn't endure it any longer, the three men stopped at an intersection. When I caught up, I introduced myself and asked if I could join them. A very tall man caught my attention and welcomed me. He turned out to be Ralph Antolino and would later become not only my dear friend, but my invaluable financial advisor.

That day was a prime example of the Universe working in my favor; when I put in the effort and showed up, amazing things happened.

We had a warm, delicious, Amish breakfast reflecting the wholesome surrounding countryside near Plain City. On our ride back to Columbus, I learned that Ralph had won a bronze medal in the Masters 40-Kilometer Time Trial at the most recent National Championships. My mom always taught me to "play up," meaning I should practice with people who were better than me at my sport. Ralph fit her description perfectly, so I planned to train with him whenever I could in the coming months and years. And, yes, I thanked my mom.

Over the next several years, Ralph and I shared racing stories and training techniques, our mutually competitive spirits finding a harmonious chord. Then, a few years later, while training for a team-time trial with another elite racer on a country road in Ohio, an SUV ran a stop sign at high speed and knocked me down – a nearly fatal impact.

I had a concussion, broken bones (in my knee, pubic bone, spine, and shoulder) and was in trauma care and rehabilitation for seven weeks. I learned a new definition of "getting up" when medical professionals predicted I would never ride again. *(More about this in Chapter Seven.)*

But I couldn't abide by that; I couldn't envision a life without riding. My communities showed up for me – my cycling friends, my church, my family, and my co-workers. They lifted me until I could stand on my own. My closest friend even put me on the back of a tandem bicycle until I could balance on my own bike again.

Focused on completely regaining my life and skills, I experienced a new combination of building physical health, emotional wellness, and financial wealth, a combination that I call **Emotional Wellth**. Over the following years, I realized I was viewing life through a new framework for resilience which I present here in ***Antidote***.

My friend Ralph introduced me to a way of thinking about money that transformed my mindset from scarcity to one of means. I had to "rethink" my financial circumstances. When that was successful**,** I realized I wanted to apply this rethinking to other parts of my life as well.

A chance meeting on a country road led me to discover new strengths in times of crisis. The stories in ***Antidote*** name seven special resources that helped me heal and move forward. I call these **Emotional Bank Accounts**. These personal and professional resources help me now as I deal with the inevitable unexpected challenges of everyday life. Unwittingly, I had made "deposits" into my "accounts" through caring communication and active group support. These sincere connections gave me purpose and helped me build resilience.

I learned I could draw from these accounts in times of need.

When I first sent my thoughts on six **Emotional Bank Accounts** to my mom, she said, "John, this is great, but you're missing one."

I wasn't surprised. She always pushed me to higher levels.

"What am I missing, Mom?"

"A dream bank," she stated simply. And as I considered her comment, I realized she was right.

From the dreams we envision for our lives, we gain **Emotional Wellth**.

"Dreams play a central role in your emotional equilibrium," she continued. "Without the aspiration of your dreams, you're not inspired to pursue them. And once you are inspired, you must sweat to make them happen."

Disability, Disillusionment and Depression

As I reflected on her words, I realized that after my setbacks, I had fallen into a saddened state of mind. I felt mentally paralyzed, mirroring my physical disability. My brother, a medical doctor, came to my bedside in the rehab hospital.

"I don't have any doubt that your bones will heal," he said. "I've seen you get up again and again after crashing through all the years you've been bike racing." He let that sink in. Then he said something that brought me to tears.

"I worry more that your persona of a champion cyclist will never be the same."

For the first time since the accident, I had to confront the possibility that he was right. The shadow of doubt cast by this sudden change to the course of my life had been lingering behind my obvious new physical limitations. I had invested so much of my identity into the world of competitive bike racing, who would I actually *be* if I couldn't race? Who would I be if I couldn't ride a bike?

Was it possible that without these things, I no longer knew who I was?

"Bro, you always have a way of getting to the core of an issue," I sighed through my tears. "It's not just the setback of these broken bones that makes me so sad. It's slowly coming to an awareness of something bigger. It's the possibility that the joy I've always felt from training and racing may be gone forever."

At that moment, that potential was devastating to me.

A broken bone heals, but how do you heal a broken ego?

My community of friends helped me realize I needed to discard the predictions that didn't align with my dreams. My years of believing in my friends led them to return that energy to me. They believed in me!

After seven weeks in the rehab hospital, I returned to Virginia. I was speaking with my dear friend from my church, Jim Long. Just eight weeks after the accident, the church had invited me to speak to all my church friends.

"Jim, although I want to thank the congregation for the prayer quilt and so many get-well cards, every time I try to say it, I come to tears. I don't think I can get through it. Maybe it's too soon?"

"JC, I'll pick you up tomorrow and take you to church. Let's see what happens, okay?"

Jim arrived at my apartment that Sunday morning and helped me get to his car on my crutches. I wanted to sit in the back of the church in case I couldn't make it through the service. When we got there, he walked me to the front pew and put the crutches under the seat and sat next to me.

"When it's time for you to speak, I'll get you to the pulpit." He was unwavering in his belief that I would be able to share my message of gratitude with our congregation, who had cared for me in my time of need. He got me up there. I took a deep breath, gripped the podium and spoke clearly from my heart. No tears. A "God" wink.

Like Jim, my other groups of friends helped me rethink my circumstances. They helped me let go of thoughts, behaviors, and habits that led to inactivity, self-doubt and isolation. Their loving care helped me see that the accident had pushed me into what I call "the arc of loneliness." I needed to emerge into a new **Emotional Wellth** through meaningful engagement with others.

I discovered that my tacit contributions to other people's lives over many years yielded a strong belief in myself. Whenever things weren't turning out the way I dreamed they would, I found that I could check in with friends to get back on track.

This is my story of healing in degrees, all because of who I was before the crash. I had made deposits through participation and caring, building a wealth that I never knew existed, wealth that I could draw on to heal from a massive setback.

I encourage you to pause after each story, taking three minutes to write down:

- How you give
- How you love
- How you praise
- How you learn

...and more, to help you see that you already have a positive balance.

The **_Antidote_** stories are not prescriptive methods to earn a balance in your own **Emotional Wellth** accounts. But this book invites you to recognize your own positive Wellth, understanding that these accounts are resources in times of challenge. Each crisis that befalls you reveals a path to a new resilience. I hope this book helps you discover the positive balance that is already there in your **Emotional Bank Accounts**.

Emotional Wellth Framework™

This book describes how I healed. The **Emotional Wellth Framework** is called "**Antidote**" because no doctor could prescribe it; no nurse could inject it to heal me. _The antidote is that I had the power to heal within me. I had a positive balance in my emotional bank accounts to draw upon._

Only in my heart could I know if I was whole again. The toughest part for my ego was believing in myself again. The **Framework**, once revealed to me, helped me see how others believed in me: friends, family, colleagues, my church choir, fellow cyclists and rowers each showed me the path to recover my balance.

Imagine you're walking in the woods, and you come across a small reflecting pool. In it, you see a soul stronger than you ever thought possible. That is the _you_ which you may encounter using the **Emotional Wellth Framework** presented here. Perhaps this book will give you the courage to look into your own accounts to see your hidden **Emotional Wellth** through your life stories.

I realized that my emotional assets enabled me to bounce out of hardship and loneliness with hope and healing. You may discover that a spiritual connection, social engagement, deep fitness, financial planning, a life of learning, giving back, and your dreams give you a new start. These resources enabled me to return to an active life again from painful loss and injury. The stories in **Antidote** are about events that tested my "emotional balance" in each area, requiring me to dive deep into myself to summon what I needed to survive and thrive.

Chartered psychologist and sports coach Sarah Broadhead explains that resilience is the ability to continue to function when you are under pressure. She says we are not born with this skill. Whether in life or in sports, we can all improve our thoughts and feelings and turn to our support network of friends and family, learning when to stop and recover. I add prayer and gratitude to these.

Antidote is all of these factors combined and not any one of them standing alone. Because we are holistic humans, our strengths are many-faceted. Each of the accounts provides personal and professional resources that are inextricably intertwined for good. When I encountered a crisis, my awareness grew that I could tap into my **Emotional Wellth** accounts. My own resilience had come from investing time and caring for others in these seven specific areas of my life long before I needed it.

Here are the seven areas of the **Emotional Wellth Framework**:

Emotional Wellth Framework™

DREAM: Dreams are central to everything else in our lives. They give us something to live for. When we clearly name our dreams, we gain superpowers that enable us to get back on track after a crisis. Having a clear picture of our aspirations helps us to check in and reorient ourselves when we get knocked off course or things don't feel right.

HEALTH: We can build self-confidence through exercise. This gives us a well of health to draw upon when we get sick or suffer a crisis. Deep immersion training can lead to extraordinary performances. Peak health and conditioning can become a source of resilience to overcome perceptions of inadequacy, or to recover from a setback.

LEARNING: A life of learning leads to a healthy posture toward our changing world. By rethinking each circumstance, we can learn our way out of almost any corner. We grow this asset when we engage in learning and problem-solving. We can tap new resources to let go of old beliefs that may be holding us back and then realize our full inner resourcefulness.

EARNING: Perhaps our most emotional resource is our financial readiness. When we get this right, we create a "get out of jail" card that we can play when a crisis falls into our path. Learning the "ABC's of Money" can keep us safe, hopeful, and more able to bounce back.

GIVING: Gratitude and thanks can take the form of giving your time or your resources. In 2022, we Americans gave nearly $500 billion to charity, with $319 billion of that from individuals. Selfless giving lifts people up. Giving with purpose can grow our hearts in a win-win for both givers and receivers.

LOVE: The more you give to your relationships, the more likely people will show up for you in times of need. Research shows that "social integration" is the key to longevity. Amazingly, this emotional quotient is more valuable than intelligence and plays a stronger role than genetics, exercise and nutrition! When we engage with friends, we benefit from caring and receiving care. Sharing coffee and caring builds a stronger community, mind and body.

SPIRIT: When we lift a weight, it's easy to demonstrate and measure our physical strength. Similarly, we have the opportunity to strengthen our spiritual connection in the mission field of life every day. When we do, we gain transformative resources of community and faith to withstand a crisis.

Please join me for a ride into a new emotional framework for your life. Instead of falling apart when a crisis occurs and spiraling down into loneliness, build **Emotional Wellth** that can lift you up again and again. Discover the power of your personal resilience - at any age - by building your **Emotional Bank Accounts,** which you can then rely on forever in times of need.

Enjoy the ride!

JC Chamberlain, Sr

Chapter 1
Dream Wellth

"Life is too short to wake up in the morning with regrets. You're in pretty good shape for the shape you're in."

Dr. Seuss

Think BIG, work small. I rode my bicycle 60,000 miles over five years for my dream of winning a 60-minute race. I was able to achieve big milestones in my life by going deep into the details of my training. When a personal disaster occurred, I had to quickly assess how to recover and move on. By focusing on my BIG dreams instead of my setbacks, I found the way to get on track again. I learned that **Dream Wellth** comes from dreaming big and working small to achieve my goals.

Dream BIG, Work Small

A friend and fellow cyclist, Kevin, runs training camps for college basketball players who are preparing for their six-week-long tryouts with NBA teams. These are intense physical trials that pave the critical path for recruitment into a professional basketball career. Based on your performance, teams decide if they will select you – or not.

One day when we were riding together, I asked Kevin, "Can your program be applied to cycling?"

"Hmm. Well, JC, cycling is an endurance sport that takes hours and hours of riding," he answered. "On the other hand, professional basketball requires bursts of energy, sprinting from one end of the court to the other and only totals 48 minutes over four periods."

"Let me put it another way," I asked. "What if my event was only one hour?"

"Okay, now we have something to talk about. What is this event anyway?"

"It's called the *Hour Record,* a capstone race against the clock to cover the most distance in an hour on a bicycle. It's one of the most sought after individual time trial records in cycling."

"Then, yes, my program could be adapted to train for that. I would break it into four 15-minute segments of intense but varied efforts."

"Game on, brother!"

Kevin customized his workouts for cycling, and we began to train together. He tested my performance quarterly. The record attempt was to be on a high-altitude cycling track called a velodrome to take advantage of the one-second per lap advantage you get by racing in thinner air. I decided to race on the Olympic Velodrome in Mexico City where Eddy Merckx, winner of five Tour de France, set the Hour Record in 1972.

His herculean effort began a decades-long battle by a throng of athletes to extend that distance. His record was broken 29 times on that track, including once by Merckx himself!

Records like this are made to be broken. I was totally comfortable with this. To hold a world record for *any* amount of time would achieve my *biggest* dream.

After two years of intense training with Kevin, one day he handed me Malcolm Gladwell's blockbuster book, *Outliers*. He said, "Gladwell has a rule of thumb that goes like this: It takes 10,000 hours of intensive practice to achieve mastery of complex skills and materials. This is like Itzhak Perlman playing the violin or getting as good as Bill Gates at software. I would be interested to know if you see yourself in this book."

I have always practiced deep immersion to become the best at something. Whether it was violin or baseball or cycling, I always threw myself into training with everything I had. After reading Gladwell's book, I realized I might *be* an outlier.

Out came a pad of paper and a pencil: By 2009, I had raced 1,050 races. I had won a medal or a trophy in 250 of these races beginning in 1972. I had been riding since 1970 and covered a little over 200,000 miles. At an average of 20 miles per hour, I calculated that I had put in Gladwell's magic number of 10,000 hours of preparation.

Ahh, but how long would it take me now, in my 50s, to return to the professional level of cycling? I figured that was the level I would need to reach in order to set a world record.

I was working full-time, so Kevin had me hitting the gym at 6 AM and 6 PM every day. It was humbling and hard: It took five years, 50 more races, and 60,000 miles of cycling to get ready.

One day, while I was training, my son Chris said a startling thing to me: "Dad, you are *"whole"* ass."

I was taken aback. "Excuse me?"

He beamed. "Because you don't do anything *half*-ass!"

He had me there. We both grinned at his revelation.

I had many challenges as I was growing up. Chris knew that when I had rheumatic fever as a four-year-old, I had refused to be hospitalized – because all I knew at that age was that people died in hospitals. My fever broke and I was allowed to stay home. However, I developed a heart murmur when one of my valves didn't heal from the serious infection. I was prescribed bicillin, a penicillin antibiotic, to prevent a relapse of the disease.

We lived on Staten Island, in New York. In 1961, the only way our family could afford the bicillin was to go to a clinic at Columbia University, where we went once a month for my shot. My mother and I took the Staten Island ferry to Battery Park in Manhattan. We walked from the ferry docks to the uptown subway and rode 124 blocks north to Columbia.

The bicillin shot was a large needle in my butt cheek. It was painful, and caused a rash, making me limp for days. I grew to fear anything in a needle. Ultimately, I had to be held down by four people to get the shots because I dreaded them so much. And I had to have an EKG every year. During those years, the EKG was always bad news: I still had a leaky heart valve.

I was told by doctors that I would never be able to do sports because of the murmur.

That is a terrible thing for a little boy to hear. All I wanted was a baseball glove and bat!

Mom took me and my brother to other homes to play when she learned that their kids had the mumps, measles or chickenpox. This was her way to immunize us to diseases for which there was no vaccine yet. Her plan was to strengthen us before we went out into the world. On one occasion, I met a young girl visiting from New Jersey named Frederica Von Stade, who had the mumps. She got through them, because later she became a soloist with the Metropolitan Opera in New York City. Sure enough, I got the mumps.

At age seven, I begged my parents to buy me a violin. They said no but agreed to rent one. I started to practice three hours a day. I challenged my way to the first seat in the first violin section of my middle school orchestra. At age 14, when I applied to Taliesin, the Frank Lloyd Wright school in Wisconsin, they asked to hear me play as part of the interview. And I got in!

At home, my mom was struggling to reconcile her genius IQ with a very low self-esteem. She was clinically depressed. One day, I came home from school and a police car was in the driveway. They had found mom in the countryside tangled up in a barbed wire fence.

She was committed to a local hospital where they could monitor her closely while she recovered. Dad was traveling a lot for his work, so we always had a sitter. We visited Mom on weekends, and she returned home after a few months. But then dad moved out and they were divorced by the time I was 10.

My brother Allan was my rudder during these early years. He just seemed to know things. He was already sure that he was going to be a doctor when he grew up. Mom was high functioning, yet still quite depressed. She had a small stipend from The Ohio State University where she was a graduate student in the Department of Education. It was not much. We bought most of our food at a co-op on campus. Mom made weekly menus and we cooked for ourselves before she came home from her long days at school. Dad mailed a check for $125 a month from his new home in California.

I've always felt inspired by my family heritage, which encouraged me to know myself and not be directed by stranger's expectations.

My granddad James P. Mayo, Sr. came from a line of revolutionaries. His mother was a suffragist and among those women who picketed the White House in 1918 for the right to vote. She was jailed during that protest. Her great uncle was a Massachusetts farmer who served as the model for the "Minute Man" statue in Lexington Common. These were the early patriots who were prepared to fight for liberty with one minute of notice, and who rallied to fight the British on the night of Paul Revere's famous ride.

When my great grandmother returned from Washington, she told the local paper in Framingham, Massachusetts "I hope there will be a revolutionary in each generation of my family."

Indeed!

My life as a sick child began to transition thanks to baseball and a bicycle. My grandparents sent me a $20 bill in the mail for my 10th birthday. I decided it was their way of telling me – without telling me – that I could play sports even if the doctors said I should not. So I used it to buy a catcher's mitt and three official leather Major League baseballs. I threw the skins off those three baseballs that spring.

I wanted the chance to throw a real runner out at second base.

I had a *big* dream and used my passion to practice every day. And that was my ticket into sports! Since the catcher didn't run much, Mom let me try out for the Worthington Little League. Her rationale was that crouching behind home plate would not stress my heart. She bought me a one-speed bike to get to practice. I loved that bike and rode it everywhere; it was my first freedom.

After the divorce, Mom wanted to bring our single-parent family together with an exciting summer vacation. We didn't have much money, but she found a travel book titled *Europe on $5-A-Day*, and we spent the winter months planning a bicycling trip around Britain and France, while staying in youth hostels. My grandfather helped us buy new 10-speed bikes, only asking that my brother and I each earn $100 to contribute to the total. I mowed lawns and shoveled walkways, and Allan delivered the morning paper in our neighborhood.

That trip would change my life forever.

We signed onto a charter flight in Toronto, Canada and put the bikes on the plane with us. Four huge propellers powered us across the Atlantic Ocean. I was glued to the window most of the way and for hours it seemed that we were only a few hundred feet off the moonlit waves.

One of the attractions for me as a thirteen-year-old, was that there were "hippies" in the back row of the airplane with long hair not that different from my own shoulder-length hair. During the flight, they passed a "glowing pin" among themselves and I was able to stand nearby to breathe in its sweet smell. Back at my seat, I drifted off into a deep sleep and woke up as we landed at Gatwick Airport in London.

We reassembled our bicycles, attached our saddle bags, and headed for the Youth Hostel at Charing Cross in London. I was promptly stopped by a "Bobby" policeman. He blew his whistle at me for riding on the wrong side of the road! In London, Piccadilly, Buckingham Palace, Big Ben, St. Paul's Cathedral and Westminster Abbey all enthralled us. Then we rode out to Stonehenge. In all, we rode a 100-mile radius of London staying each night in an inexpensive youth hostel. Then we took a boat train to Boulogne-sur-Mer, France and bicycled east to Paris.

I was captivated by the monuments, churches, and museums. We rode south through the Loire Valley with its scenic river. Each city had an extraordinary cathedral, chateau, gardens, and a "sound and light" show in the evening to tell the history of the city, church or castle. I was exposed to Renaissance architecture, outdoor lighting, and French culture by immersion.

Each of these had a profound impact on me, clearly, as I chose to study architecture in college and became an outdoor-lighting expert. I became fluent in French and later had a French business partner.

We sure traveled light on that trip! We each had a summer-weight, down sleeping bag and a "sheet sleeping sack" made from parachute material. At the youth hostels, they gave you a bed, and a blanket. It was expected that we use the "sleeping sack" to keep the blankets clean from one guest to another. This all seemed to work just fine and made it possible for these friendly overnight places to operate very inexpensively.

The only non-essential thing I brought from home was my ping-pong paddle. It became my essential task each day when we arrived at the "Auberge de Jeunesse" (youth hostel in French) to find the local ping-pong table, which turned out to be a perfect way to socialize and meet people.

I had studied French in school for only one year before we arrived. A good start. At the ping-pong table and on our travels, I learned more French that summer by watching people form their language, and then imitating how they held their lips, face, and the pace with which they said their words. Soon I, too, began to sound like the French.

Mom insisted that we wear cycling jerseys with American flag patches. It was heartwarming to experience how French families welcomed us as we met them along our tour. We corresponded with one family every year. They would write to Mom in French. I would translate it, and she would compose a reply. I would write it in French, and she would copy it into her own hand. It was great practice for me, and we traded holiday greetings this way for several decades.

We rode the entire perimeter of France, into Andorra, Switzerland and Germany, returning to London via Amsterdam. It was a 2,200-mile amateur Tour de France that we accomplished in 42 days, a comparison not lost on me.

One day in Rouen, France I met Eddy Merckx, who had just won a stage of the 21-day professional Tour de France riding solo at 28 miles per hour ahead of the peloton. I squeezed my way to the front of the crowd and shook his hand. He was a superstar and this 13-year-old wanted to connect with his energy. It was just one year later that he set his first Hour Record.

Oh, the influence that handshake had on my cycling career!

In 2011, 41 years later, Merckx and I met again at the Classic Car Club Manhattan. Merckx was in the U.S. to celebrate the 50th Anniversary of *Bicycling Magazine*. At the behest of Rodale Press, the founders of the magazine, he was signing autographs. My coach for the Hour Record attempt was Jack Simes, a third generation professional cyclist, and an Olympic and World Champion. Through a mutual friend, Jack had arranged for me to meet Merckx.

I eagerly awaited my turn. With me was the one-piece aerodynamic skinsuit I planned to wear during my attempt to break his record. I was excited to reconnect with him to share the impact he had on my cycling. I spoke to him in French. Being Belgian, he was amused. He listened intently as I made my request: "If you sign my jersey over my heart, I will carry your strength with me for the hour."

He responded in perfect English: "Your French is very good. And, yes, I will sign it. I wish you the very best of luck," he added demurely. "I hope the record is broken again and again." Then he asked me to sit right next to him for a picture of us shaking hands, 41 years after we had first shook hands in France.

After our European trip, our little family of three had become thrilled and encouraged about the possibilities for inexpensive travel that long-distance cycling offered. During the next winter, we planned to ride from Seattle to Boston the following summer. We wrote to every state to check their laws about teenagers cycling alone. As a result, we each carried a $20 bill with a permission note and phone numbers of our parents. We obtained the AAA TourBooks for our route across the country. We mailed our reservations to campgrounds and to families we planned to stay with along the way. We designed and built our own tents.

Mom taught us that if we dreamed BIG, planned, and took action, we could accomplish nearly anything. In 1979, for example, I started my first business by sewing ballistic nylon into bicycle travel bags. Known as the "Chamberlain SkyBag," my first stock-held startup manufactured 4,000 bicycle travel bags over the next five years. This created a new category of equipment in the bicycling industry that is still an active product segment today.

My mother, brother and I got certified to lead our cycling trip through the American Youth Hostels Leadership Training

Program. At age 14, I was the youngest person ever to complete the training. We brought on three other cyclists our age, whose parents paid for the whole trip. One family donated a car that Mom drove across the country with our camping gear and a spare bike.

During that 4,000-mile bike ride, I entered my first bike race at a cycling rally in Ohio. My brother coached me on when to start my sprint. After training for 3,000 miles over the past 30 days, I won the 15-mile race easily.

I learned I was coachable, and that with deep immersion training I could win!

After that first success, Allan found a local bicycle racing club in our hometown of Columbus, Ohio and we began to race three or more times every week. That year, I won my age group in the Ohio-West Virginia region for road racing as well as a series of oval track races. And I won the next year, and the next one, too. I was riding 400 miles a week. I loved it!. After years of being told I could *not* do sports, I felt like an uncaged bird.

Looking back on those years now, I can see it all started with $20 and three baseballs.

A senior in our racing club named Gregg, who was also an Ohio State Champion, began to mentor me. Two top racers in our club, Ted and Bill, were four years older than me, and they agreed to include me in their training and racing. They became National Champions and even went to the Pan-American Games.

This gave me elite-level role models to train with every day. Gregg encouraged me to train for the National Championships in Milwaukee. This was a BIG goal. Mom knew she couldn't afford the expense of driving hundreds of miles a week to the regional qualification races. We needed financial help to supplement my training. Mom encouraged me to talk to her brother. I called my uncle on the phone and stuck to a script I had prepared because I was nervous about it.

"Uncle Jimmy, Mom said to ask you if you will help me get to the races so I can qualify for nationals."

His response came quickly as though he had already thought about it. Perhaps she had tipped him off to pave the way for my call?

"I will help, but only if you write down all the races you plan to enter and the expenses you'll incur to get there."

I mapped out 25 races that had entry fees. I added tires and equipment, gas, hotels and meals for races held in other cities. I figured I could ride to the local mid-week track and road races throughout most of the year. It came to a total of about 100 races each year.

"We'll use your list to create a budget," Jimmy told me. "You'll keep track of the expenses during the year. And we'll see how accurate your prediction is. This is what we call a budget."

Jimmy was a buyer at the MIT Lincoln Laboratory. He also taught me about his "aging" drawer. Here he would put prices for things he didn't need to buy yet. I learned from him that usually the longer you wait to buy something, the lower the price gets.

Jimmy, who clearly cared about me, stepped in as my surrogate dad to teach me how to forecast expenses, create a budget, and then measure my results. He made me keep receipts and I tracked my training and racing in handwritten logs from the very beginning. He made me stick to the budget. And I applied these new skills to my training, too.

I went on to win a handful of significant races, including a Silver Medal in the 50-mile National Road Race in my age group. This fueled my self-confidence and bolstered my physical health. The once-sickly kid was doing okay!

I crashed over 100 times in my career. That's just part of the sport of bicycle racing; it's how you get up that matters most. Mom always asked, "Is the bike okay?" She seemed to intuitively understand that she could patch us up later, but we could only finish the race if the bike was still able to go on.

34 years later, in 2009, I was working on my strength and fitness every morning following the plan put in place by Kevin. Most days, I rode 50 miles after work and put in longer rides or races on the weekends. After my divorce, I had moved from my 7,000 square foot home on five acres to a one-room rental of 100-square feet with access to a kitchen and living area. The apartment was near a regional rail trail, at least, so I could ride during rush hour without hitting traffic. My daily fitness focus kept me on track to my **BIG** dream.

One day, after my ride, I showered and was going to rest in my room before going downstairs to prepare dinner. A strong intuition led me to hesitate, and I decided to tidy up the bathroom. Suddenly, while I was in the bathroom, I heard a thundering sound from behind me in the direction of my bedroom. What the hell?

I came out of the bathroom and the door to my room was closed. I had to push with all my might to open it a crack. The ceiling had fallen down onto my bed! Insulation and drywall covered everything I could see. I had placed a small cross on the wall above my desk. The nail and cross now held a piece of the ceiling just a few inches above a picture of my son under the lamp on my desk.

It was a small glimmer of hope in the midst of this new chaos.

It was three days before the state track cycling championships at a velodrome near Allentown Pennsylvania. I felt numb. At first, I felt short of breath. Then, I wanted to cry. I gulped a steadying breath, grabbed my duffle bag and walked downstairs, where I found an envelope from the day's mail. Sitting on the bottom step next to my bike, I drafted an action plan to recover from this disaster.

I began by listing five families I knew whom I thought might take me in on short notice. Most were friends from my Boy Scout community where I had been involved as an adult leader over the past six years. Then I called my mom. She knew everything and everyone in my life up to this moment. (She always called herself my "Number One Fan.") I filled her in, had a good cry in my despair, then hung up to start making calls. I left two messages – and then my phone rang.

"My brother!" came Sarah's voice. Sarah is the sister I never had. We were working together on a virtual fitness coaching business she had created and she chose my mom to be her U.S. mom.

"I emptied my Mercedes, and I am on the way to pick you up with whatever you need for three days. And I'll be there in fifteen minutes." In her broken English/Iranian accent, she added "Our 'mudder,'" meaning my mom, "called and said to come right away because you had a crisis. See you soon." Click.

Salvation! I made a list of what I needed for the upcoming race weekend, squeezed into my room, packed my things, and stayed at Sarah's for the next two days.

I went to Pennsylvania for the championships, where I won five gold, two silver and three bronze medals in my events. In spite of the crisis — perhaps even motivated by it — and by checking in with my BIG dreams, I stayed on track.

Later that year, I went to Los Angeles instead of Mexico City where there's a world class indoor velodrome. On the day of my Hour Record attempt, my time was only three-quarters of a second per lap *off* the world record time, groan!

Yet, the distance of 26.1 miles was a *personal record* for me and just under a mile less than Merckx rode in 1972.

I was not discouraged. I'd had some unusual setbacks along the way — physical and financial challenges, a divorce, the ceiling literally falling in — but I kept my vision on my BIG goal.

Dream Wellth™ in Action

Think BIG, work small. I rode my bicycle 60,000 miles over five years for my dream of winning a 60-minute race. I was able to achieve big milestones in my life by going deep into the details of my training. When the ceiling of my rental crashed down, I had to quickly assess how to recover and move on. By focusing on my BIG dreams instead of my setbacks, I found the way to get on track again. I learned that **Dream Wellth** comes from dreaming big and working small to achieve my goals. #dreamwellth

Big Picture - Zoom Out

The pursuit of big dreams, like setting the Hour Record in cycling, requires not just ambition but a strategic and disciplined approach. By aiming high and breaking down the journey into manageable parts, you can achieve extraordinary feats. This story demonstrates that with dedicated planning, effort and a resilient attitude, even the loftiest goals are within reach.

Dream Wellth aims to inspire you to dream big and understand the profound satisfaction that comes from transforming seemingly impossible aspirations into reality.

The bigger idea here is the power of **deep immersion, strategic planning, and unwavering commitment** in achieving significant milestones. It's about setting a monumental goal and understanding that every small step contributes to the grand achievement.

This approach transcends cycling and can be applied to any field or personal ambition. The essence is to think big, break down the journey into smaller, actionable steps, and stay committed through challenges and setbacks. My story underscores that both mental and physical preparation, combined with a support system, are crucial for success.

Tactics – Ideas to Action

Consider these tactics to transform big dreams into tangible achievements, one small, deliberate step at a time:

Set a Monumental Goal (Think Big):

☐ Define a clear, ambitious goal that excites and challenges you.

☐ Examine it to ensure that it aligns with your real passions and long-term aspirations.

Break Down the Goal (Work Small):

☐ Divide the larger goal into smaller, achievable segments.

☐ For example, if your goal is to write a book, break it down into chapters, and then pages per day.

Engage Expert Guidance:

- ☐ Seek out mentors or coaches who have experience in the field of your goal.
- ☐ Customize your training or learning program to fit your specific needs, much like Kevin adapted his basketball training to cycling.

Implement Consistent Training/Practice:

- ☐ Develop a training schedule that fits into your daily routine.
- ☐ Commit to regular practice or training sessions to build up to your goal gradually.

Track Progress and Adapt:

- ☐ Keep detailed logs of your progress and periodically assess your performance.
- ☐ Make necessary adjustments to your training or your approach based on these evaluations.

Embrace Resilience:

- ☐ Prepare for setbacks and learn to view them as part of the journey.
- ☐ Develop a mindset that sees challenges as opportunities to grow and improve.

Build a Support System:

- ☐ Surround yourself with supportive friends, family, or a team who understand your goal and can provide encouragement.
- ☐ Communicate regularly with your support system about your progress and challenges.

Stay Motivated:

- ☐ Remind yourself regularly of your ultimate goal and why it matters to you.

- ☐ Celebrate small victories along the way to maintain motivation and momentum.

Your Turn ✎

What are your BIG dreams?

How do you visualize and plan to reach your goals?

From a setback, what motivates you to keep going?

How could the outcome here have been very different?

How can you "work small" to reach your BIG goals?

Chapter 2
Health Wellth

"The struggle for today is not altogether for today – it is for a vast future also."

Abraham Lincoln

A lack of spending money that made me different from my peers caused me to "row over" the Gamut Erg at the boathouse on weekends instead of going to social club parties. Soon, the whole team was there – in deep immersion training. Scientific studies reveal that regular exercise releases myokines, a protein that improves mental health and resilience and decreases inflammation. Whatever your age, there's strong scientific evidence that being physically active can help you lead a healthier and happier life. As it turned out, this **Health Wellth** and sports-training strategy had the surprise byproduct of allowing me to overcome my perceived social shortcomings.

No Beer Money

Being from a middle-class family at an Ivy League university was humbling in many ways. From the minute I arrived on campus, I was tripping over my own shortcomings. I didn't have corduroys or loafers, like the other students; I wore jeans and clogs. My parents didn't hold positions on Wall Street or in Washington. I struggled with these social setbacks in my life.

The legacy students at Princeton, who often came from generations of Princeton alumni, caused me the most consternation. They had grown up with the means to afford Princeton. They assumed admission and acceptance by their peers would be automatic.

There are no athletic scholarships in the Ivy League; I had loans and grants. To be sure, there were always money challenges. Even the cost of textbooks, room, board, and travel were daunting for me. I worked in the student union as a short-order cook and then became the manager. It was an added effort to balance my work-study jobs (awarded in exchange for the scholarships I received).

In my sophomore year, it was my invitation to join Ivy Club, an all-male eating club and bastion of legacy families, that created an opportunity to learn from these kids. I hesitated to accept it – would I fit in? And I worried about the cost of membership. It was a challenge, but I decided I would need to work with these young men throughout my adult life, so I took the bid. And by keeping my family apprised of the reasons for my choice, I rallied enough financial support to get through the next couple of years.

Sitting with my fellow members at meals and around the club, I tried to question their way of thinking, to help them see another point of view. I wanted to understand what made them think the way they did. Some of my clubmates were too absorbed in their future career path to engage with me.

However, others were open and listened and challenged me in return. I was surprised to discover that they might not adhere to the family traditions that had fueled my perceptions in the first place. For example, one son of a prominent Chicago banking family chose the ministry instead of following in his father's footsteps. I learned to see the world through their eyes. And we grew in our mutual respect for each other. Several of these became lifelong friendships.

I aspired to compete in the 1980 Moscow Olympics as a cyclist. I joined the small cycling team, becoming the captain. Cycling is the oldest organized sport in the Ivy League. I rode everywhere on campus and into the surrounding countryside. My position of leadership took a lot of administrative time, as I was organizing meetings, going to races and fundraising.

I needed to re-focus on my long-term goal of the Olympics.

After my sophomore year, I took a leave of absence to train exclusively for endurance road racing. In 1980, my training included a camp at the Olympic Training Center in Colorado Springs. The Russians invaded Afghanistan in December of 1979, resulting in President Carter deciding to boycott the Moscow Games to mitigate risks to our athletes and to deny the Russians the publicity of being host. After four years of dreaming and preparation, no Olympics for me. I spent the year racing, and then returned to school.

During this time, making the Varsity Rowing Team brought into focus all of my years of training for bicycle racing. I had worked so hard to prepare for the 1980 Olympic year, yet those dreams had evaporated in front of my eyes. Naturally, this frustrated me, and I was immensely disappointed. When I returned to school that fall, rowing emerged as an outlet for my frustration. I had a new target for my competitiveness that morphed into the collaboration required to succeed in eight-oared rowing.

We were a Lightweight Crew. This meant that we had to average 155 pounds every Friday to "weigh in" before our Saturday races against other schools. I sensed that some of the guys were distracted and always seemed to be preoccupied with their future career in law, medicine or business. As an antidote, I began to visit our boat after practice and learned that I could sense the energy left there by each of my teammates. It felt like they were trying too hard. I encouraged them to let go of trying to do it all themselves when we trained together.

"Think of the energy in the boat as though it is flowing through a pipe," I said. "You are in there with all of us, giving it 100%." Some would just look at me in disbelief. But a few listened.

"Then let yourself relax," I said. "Give 90% instead of 100%. Let the power of an external force, a universal power, come into the pipe to give you the extra 10%. Let that force lift you so you feel it is easier to do your part. See what happens."

Some guys did not seem to respond to this, but I knew it to be true from my own experience, so I shared my philosophy with each member of my boat. The result was that we started to be very competitive with the other varsity teams. The Heavyweight Crews outweighed us by fifty pounds per rower on average. That's a lot of muscle! Yet, we were able to hold our own for more than 1500 meters of a 2,000-meter race with them.

I knew we were onto something. The net result was that we rowed better together. And we trained exceptionally hard. This put us in a strong position versus teams from other schools. With this endurance and strength preparation, we could focus on moving in harmony with the shell, oars, water, and each other.

The outcome was extraordinary!

We were undefeated and won the Eastern Sprints, the de facto national championship, in a record-setting time.

When I arrived back at Princeton in the fall of 1980, I had been training six hours a day at the elite level of U.S. cycling. I was riding 400 miles every week. An Andover classmate, Chris, asked me one Saturday if I would like to "steal a boat," and row with him during the Columbia-Princeton football game.

"The game is gonna suck, and I can get us into the boathouse," he urged.

He used his student ID to jimmy the lock on the main door. I was impressed by his streetwise savvy. Once in, we found what is known as a "straight pair." This is the *most* difficult boat to row in all of rowing. First, there is no coxswain, so the bowman must steer the boat by turning the toe of his shoe, which is literally attached by wires to the rudder, and occasionally he must look over his shoulder to see ahead.

This boat is outfitted for only two rowers, each with a 12-foot oar. The oarsmen must balance the boat using their hand levels – with very slight up and down movements – while moving forward and back on sliding seats through an arc of about six feet and managing to feather the oar on each stroke. "Feathering," allows the oar blade to slip through the wind between strokes. Once the oar is "squared up," each rower drops the blade into the water again and "pulls through" to complete the stroke, thus, powering the boat forward.

There was a steady drizzle falling on Lake Carnegie. The raindrops created a sea of circles as we lightly paddled up the lake. It was as though the surface was alive with waterbugs skimming along with us. As we rowed, we could hear the football game announcer from the nearby stadium.

Judging from the lack of cheers, we were indeed losing the game, so I knew we'd made the right choice.

Beginners Luck – or Was it Meant to Be?

Remarkably, the boat was perfectly set. Having never rowed this boat together before, it was surprising to me that we were balanced as we glided along through the misty rain. We rowed six miles to the end of the lake and back to the boathouse. This was quite a feat for two novices in a straight pair. I felt an elation as we coasted into the dock, even though we were soaked and my hands were blistering on the wooden oar handle.

And yet I had this feeling of bliss. With rowing, there is a gut-wrenching pain - to your hands, back and legs – and, yet, you can simultaneously be in a fluid motion on the water in harmony with each other and with nature.

Rowing coaches try hundreds of combinations - of rowers, seating, rigger settings – and never achieve what we had just experienced serendipitously.

"Hey, I'm hooked!" I announced, as we put the boat away.

"Yeah? Would you be interested in joining the team? We have a tough coach, but he may be the best coach in the boathouse right now."

"Does the team have a good record?"

He put it honestly and humbly. They were not national champions. "We've been second and fourth in the Eastern Sprints the past few years. And we haven't won the Harvard-Yale-Princeton race in 25 years. But we could be on the cusp of something great if you came on board. You want to talk with the coach to see if it would be a fit?"

On Monday, he took me to meet Coach Kilpatrick in the weightroom at the gym. We chatted. He wanted me to do an ergometer test. We all met later that day at the boathouse and I sat down on the Gamut Erg, which simulates sweep rowing.

I was familiar with this strength and endurance testing machine from training on the same machine at Andover. While the other kids were going on exotic spring vacations, I stayed on campus. It was during these formative times that my coach, Martha Beatty, used the Gamut Erg to teach me to row both starboard and port. She came to Andover from Dartmouth where she had rowed varsity, and then won a berth on the Women's National Rowing Team. She was a star, and I was fortunate to receive her personal coaching.

Today was going to be my payday.

Training Six Hours a Day Gets You Predictable Results

As a result of my ambidextrous training at Andover, it did not matter which way the oar was rigged on the erg that day. And it had been several years since my last erg test. My hands were still sore from our row in the rain on Saturday, but it felt somehow like pulling on a comfortable old sweater as I began the six-minute test. The goal was to see how many meters I could travel within the allotted time and prescribed resistance. After two minutes, the coach and Chris disappeared. I was crestfallen.

After all, I had been training and racing as a professional cyclist for the past twelve months and years of racing before that. I wondered why they had suddenly abandoned me on the erg, but I kept going.

"Do I not warrant any further attention?" a voice in my head nagged me. As the doubts swirled, I kept going because no one had told me to stop. The insecurity voice whispered, "Am I not good enough to make their team?"

About a minute later, the coach and Chris returned with what seemed like a bunch of guys who leaned in watching quietly as

I continued to row. *This* was my signal that something good was happening. Filled with adrenaline, I threw the hammer down and gave it everything I had. If nothing else, with my extensive training, I had stamina.

At the end of six minutes I had broken all previous records on that machine at Princeton! My hands were bloody, but I didn't care. And it was a treat to see the faces of the rowers gathered there. Eyeballs were rolling.

Based on these results, I was offered a seat in the first varsity boat. Of course, this shuffled the rest of the boat rosters. Princeton had *four* Varsity Lightweight crews. Over 400 athletes were on the water every day during the spring racing season. I have to admit, coming from pro-level cycling, my methods of recovery after a workout made me stick out. I wore a one-piece skinsuit because that's what cyclists were wearing to race at the international level. I didn't like the cotton shorts they handed me with no padding in the butt and the drawstring constricting my waist. I chose to ride my bicycle to warm up because running hurt my knees and cycling felt good.

Ultimately, I developed a reputation for doing what I knew worked for me. I just wanted to make a difference for my team. I hope my results pushed the teams to expect more of themselves – we all were doing something right. And Coach Kilpatrick knew how to push us higher – together.

Over the next two years, I learned about how some teammates could be more focused on their imminent medical, business or law careers than winning the next race. I learned that you don't have to be best friends with your teammates to get remarkable results. Sometimes it's better if you are *not* best friends when it comes to making hard roster decisions to win races.

The ATM is Singing the Blues – So What Shall I Do?

During my first few years of college, I would go to the ATM and there would not be enough money in my account to make even a minimal withdrawal. I worked campus jobs and started a Christmas Wreath Agency with another student, delivering the wreaths on bicycles. My mom's BP gas card got me to bicycle races. Gradually, I raised my bank balance, but maintaining it was always a struggle for me.

I was now in my junior year after taking a year off to train for Moscow. The ATM was still singing the blues and I could not seem to balance my checking account. (I wish I'd known Ralph Antolino then!) On weekends, instead of joining the eating club parties, I slipped into the boathouse using Chris's ID card trick and got on the Gamut Erg, my old friend. It had a counter to show the number of meters you rowed. The "oar" was a stub of oak about four feet long used to apply leverage to spin a flywheel. It was very "Rube Goldberg" compared to the now ubiquitous Concept 2 rowing machines. But that was all we had at the time, so I used it.

For perspective, a rowing race is 2,000 meters. A college rowing workout on the water is approximately 20,000 meters (a little over twelve miles). In about six hours, I could "row over" the counter from zero to 99,999 meters and back to zero with a rest halfway. I kept two water bottles on the floor. My testing on that machine improved, A *lot*. People wanted to know why. I shared that I had been slipping into the boathouse on weekends to row. Soon, Coach Kilpatrick set up indoor intervals on Saturdays for the whole team.

Throughout the winter months, the workouts consisted of 32 stations (eight rowers/team times four teams) making an intense effort for 60 seconds, followed by a 30-second rest, then moving to the next station. It was quite inspiring to see our collective effort. These gifted athletes had either rowed in high school or were champions in some other sport and chose to row at Princeton. Four rowers from our varsity boat qualified for the U.S. National Team and won a bronze medal at the World Championships that summer.

This team's time had come.

There is an old saying in bicycle racing that "Spring races are not won during the spring. Spring races are won during the winter." The same is even more true in collegiate rowing where the 2,000-meter racing season is in the spring. In April we traveled to Annapolis and beat Navy's first varsity boat by *eight lengths* of open water (about 32 seconds).

This was our largest margin of victory ever.

On the bus ride back, our captain, Bill, asked me, "Do you realize what we just did?"

At the time, I didn't have perspective on such a large margin of victory. After all, it was my first collegiate race. I answered, "No, what?"

Bill grinned widely and said, "We have put a *huge* target on our backs for the other schools; We're now the team to beat."

Indeed, word traveled among the Ivy League schools and our success probably spurred more than a few extra workouts for our upcoming competitors. Try as they might, we went on to an undefeated season. In a record time, we won the coveted Eastern Sprints making us the de facto national champions. This earned us the right to enter the Royal Regatta in Henley-on-Thames, England. There, some of our team met Queen Elizabeth in a once-in-a-lifetime experience.

Not having beer money turned out to be a blessing rather than a setback. My mom had taught me that if I wanted to win – and I passionately did – I needed to work harder than everyone else. With great enthusiasm, she would encourage me after a race finish by saying, "You've got to love the pain!"

So I did. I learned to love the physical and mental suffering that came with cycling and rowing performance. I have learned since, that when we exercise, our body releases a protein called myokines that are capable of crossing the blood-brain barrier. In the muscles, they reduce inflammation and improve metabolism. In the brain, they act as an antidepressant. Exercise also releases neurotransmitters such as dopamine, noradrenaline (NA), and serotonin that have a positive impact on our mood. No wonder I love it!

Health Wellth™ in Action

My Princeton experience taught me that striving has its own rewards. Perhaps it was a combination of chemistry from deep immersion in exercise, the camaraderie of my team sports, and race victories that gave me the self-confidence to overcome the differences I perceived when I arrived on campus. Over these years of cycling and rowing, I was able to turn my perceived social and financial deficits into **Health Wellth**. My extreme fitness became a real-life resource that helped me survive and thrive when I encountered setbacks. #healthwellth

Big Picture – Zoom Out

Attending an Ivy League university from a middle-class background can be humbling and revealing. It presents a unique opportunity to not just confront and overcome social differences but to use these challenges as a catalyst for personal growth and strategic advantage. By turning perceived deficits into strengths, one can develop resilience, adaptability and a winning strategy in both academics and athletics. Health Wellth serves to inspire readers to embrace their unique backgrounds and leverage them for greater personal and professional success.

The bigger idea here is the transformation of perceived social and financial disadvantages into real strengths. This narrative isn't just about fitting in at an Ivy League institution; it's about redefining what it means to belong and thrive in any competitive environment.

By focusing on health and sport training, I demonstrate that the qualities of hard work, perseverance, and adaptability can lead to extraordinary achievements. The story underscores the universal truth that our backgrounds and perceived shortcomings do not have to limit us; rather, they can propel us to greater heights when approached with the right mindset and strategy.

Tactics – Ideas to Action

By following these tactics, you'll be able to turn your unique background and perceived disadvantages into powerful assets, achieving success through a blend of resilience, strategy and determined effort.

Embrace Your Unique Background:

☐ Recognize and accept your social and financial background as part of your identity.

☐ Use your unique perspective to offer fresh insights and approaches in your field or activities.

Leverage Physical Activity for Mental and Emotional Wellbeing:

- ☐ Incorporate regular physical training or sports into your routine to build resilience and discipline.
- ☐ Use physical activity as an outlet for frustration and a source of mental clarity.

Develop a Strategic Approach to Challenges:

- ☐ Identify areas where you feel socially or financially disadvantaged and think about how you can turn these into strengths.
- ☐ Set clear, actionable goals to address these areas and take small, consistent steps toward improvement.

Engage with Different Perspectives:

- ☐ Seek out interactions with people from different backgrounds, even if it feels challenging.
- ☐ Use these interactions to understand diverse viewpoints and to learn from them.

Apply Lessons from Athletics to Other Areas:

- ☐ Apply the discipline, teamwork, and strategic thinking from sports to your academic or professional life.
- ☐ Set measurable goals and track your progress, just as you would in a training regimen.

Stay Adaptable and Open to New Opportunities:

- ☐ Be open to trying new activities or roles that might seem outside your comfort zone.
- ☐ Use setbacks as learning opportunities and stay flexible in your approach to achieving your goals.

Maintain a Positive Mindset:

- ☐ Focus on your long-term goals and remind yourself of your successes, no matter how small.

- ☐ Cultivate a mindset that sees challenges as opportunities for growth.

Build a Support Network:

- ☐ Find mentors, coaches or peers who can provide guidance and encouragement.

- ☐ Engage in communities or groups that share your interests and values.

Your Turn 🖎

Name a shortfall you turned into an advantage.

What was your first response to this obstacle?

Did you feel criticized for not being in the status quo?

Name an advantage you have over your peers.

Does that make you more sympathetic to those without it?

Do you "go it alone" or rally others to gain an advantage?

How could physical conditioning be a resource for you?

Chapter 3
Learning Wellth

**"Admit you know nothing.
Remove ego from the equation."**

*Charlie Munger, co-founder of
Berkshire Hathaway with Warren Buffet*

In today's rapidly changing world, **staying ahead of the curve requires a mindset of continuous learning and adaptation**, and a philosophy to embrace failure as a stepping stone to success. In this chapter, I lead the reader through a series of steps that have proven to yield success in early stage enterprises. I demonstrate one way to use systematic efforts in a habit of lifelong learning to achieve **Learning Wellth**.

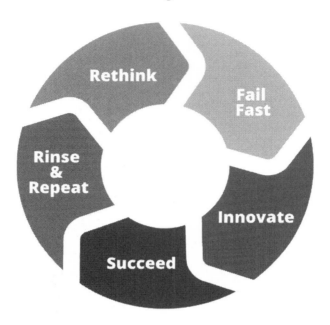

A Lifetime Learning Process

I met Bill Hambrecht at an Entrepreneur Summit in 2006 at the Princeton School of Engineering and Applied Science. We both attended Princeton as liberal arts undergraduates, only two-and-a-half decades apart. (He'd studied history and I'd studied policy.) This afforded me the insider opportunity to meet this legendary investor.

I was looking at my life through a new lens. I had concluded that I had about 15 years left to make my mark in the world of business. As you will see in the chapter on **Earning Wellth**, I had no particular retirement plan, except that I wanted to ramp up my earnings during this final phase of my work life.

Bill was a co-founder in the late 1960's of Hambrecht & Quist. They'd built a successful investment bank headquartered in San Francisco. But their culture was different from their Wall

Street counterparts; they were less regimented and more focused on innovation than more traditional investment metrics. As a student of business, I had heard of H&Q, but never imagined I could meet Mr. Hambrecht himself.

H&Q was an early player in the Internet and technology sectors. Among their most notable investments, they underwrote the Initial Public Offerings for Apple Computer, Genentech, and Adobe Systems in the 1980s. They continued their string of visionary investments and IPO's in the 1990's when they backed Netscape, MP3 and Amazon.

"We made a fortune on our positions in these early-stage companies," he began his talk. "We will never be able to do that again. This is because our old way of creating value can't compete with the new breed of company that will own the future. What they are doing I call 'ephemeralization.' They will deliver 80% of what we used to do for only 20% of the cost. The most valuable companies in the world are yet to come."

"Mr. Hambrecht, may I call you Bill?" I asked from the front row of our arena-style auditorium. There were only nine of us in the room with him.

"Please do. And what's your question?"

"Can you please name a few of these new companies?"

"Well, one of them was founded by a classmate of yours, Jeff Bezos. His company is called Amazon.com. They're turning the world of book sales on end by selling only online with no physical bricks and mortar stores. We believe they can eventually sell anything through the platform they're building."

"Please, Bill, name some more."

"One you may not have heard of yet is quickly becoming the #1 purveyor of hotel rooms. And they don't own a single hotel!

Their name is Airbnb. They simply connect you to the room you want and earn a fee in the process. Another one is breaking the traditional market for a taxi by focusing on the ride instead of the cab. That one is called Uber."

"Thank you. Fascinating! I understand you have sold H&Q, but are there breakthroughs that you're personally working on in this new era?"

"You know, I've always thought that people might want to watch football more than just in the fall. So we played around with creating digital players and teams that you can watch any time of year."

"What do you call it?"

"Well, it has kind of a whimsical name: Fantasy Football. And it seems to be taking off as we speak."

My classmates in this one-to-one with Hambrecht were also asking probing questions. Theirs were just as self-serving as mine. We were trying to quickly learn from him how to rethink our futures.

"I'll give you another example," Bill offered. "Next year, we expect Apple to come out with a phone. It will likely combine 80% of what many other devices do for just 20% of the cost. It will combine the iPod with a camera, a virtual keyboard, and it will help you navigate whether you're walking or driving. *And* it will have more memory than the Mac in a smaller package."

I could see the looks of disbelief on the faces in the room.

That was 2007 talking to us from 2006. He had a unique ability to look over the horizon to see the future. And sure enough, Apple introduced the iPhone the next year. And Amazon went on to sell pretty much everything on their platform. And Uber and Airbnb dominate their respective markets, doing more with less.

"Bill, how do we find companies with this 80/20 mindset before they are too valuable to join at the ground level?"

"Of course, that's the million-dollar question. I would say you will find plenty of opportunity by just looking for goods and services that you consider to be the most mundane things you need from day to day. Ask more questions than you answer. Get comfortable with a hunch that what you are hearing is going to make life better for a lot of people. Don't get hung up on all the details. And get involved."

We each thanked him for his generosity of time and insight into the future.

I walked out of that encounter knowing exactly what I was going to do with the rest of my life. I began immediately to look for ephemeralization in action and went hunting for the 80/20s that nobody had discovered yet.

As I ventured forth, my favorite question was: "What is the best idea you ever had that you didn't do?" And then, because God gave me two ears and one mouth, I would listen intently. And the most amazing ideas and opportunities came out. I learned that I was looking for a CEO or founder with high initiative. And I wanted to be involved with something that "did good," or produced a valued service. I wanted to be a part of something that was needed – every day – by a *lot* of people. It's easier to say no to ideas when you know precisely what you are looking for.

This was my map:

- High-initiative CEO (leadership energy)
- Produces something that creates goodwill (positive impact)
- Preserves resources/better pricing (doing more with less)
- Can scale (mass market adoption)

The Next Spring...

I met eight other cyclists in the parking lot near a caboose relic parked along a rail trail near my home. I had moved to the northern Virginia area in 1990 and continued riding but not racing. A friend from church had invited me to go on a ride with this group. To my surprise, one of my neighbors from across the street and the one next door showed up to ride as well. We all seemed to be in roughly the same age group, give or take 10 years.

As we went around the circle introducing ourselves, one guy said, "I used to race with John Chamberlain in New Jersey during the 1970's. Could that have been you?"

It was Jim. Indeed, we raced against each other in our teenage years! He was at race in Rahway when I rode 10 miles in 21:06. It was a criterium on city streets with six turns per lap. That is a nearly 30-mile-an-hour average. I broke away from the Junior field with one other rider and then won the sprint. Small world!

"If that's true, I've got a long way to go to keep up with you now."

"Very kind of you, Jim," I said, "I look forward to riding with you again today."

Another introduced himself as Christophe, with a decidedly French accent. He said he was retired from software and studying pastry with a chef in DC. I definitely wanted to learn more about that guy. We wound up at the front of the group and in conversation as we rolled along the lightly-paved rail trail. He wanted to know about my racing back in New Jersey. I said it was during high school, many moons ago.

He pressured me for more details, apparently trying to understand why Jim felt I was going to be as strong a rider today as I was in my teens. I finally shared that I had been ranked number one in the country in my age group.

He brazenly responded, "I find that hard to believe. Considering the way you're riding today, that seems very unlikely."

Naturally, I found that insulting. I have been the champion in hundreds of races, although, admittedly, now I was overweight and breathing hard. I didn't realize it at the time, but his comment unleashed something in me – he had touched a nerve. Something deep in me rose up and I found it hard to squelch a desire to show him that I was indeed a champion – once – and for all time.

That was a pivot point for me.

In the following weeks, he pestered me about joining his spinning class. We lived on opposite sides of the same nearby town. He said it was only $80 a month to join his club and then I could take all the spinning classes I wanted. I told him I didn't like spinning.

"It's too hard. Truthfully, there's no coasting, and in one hour you burn more calories than you burn on a typical 90-minute bike ride outside."

"That's the whole idea, I believe," he grinned.

Finally, I relented to try just one class with him on a Saturday.

"Let's have a coffee at the Daily Grind next door after class," he offered, as we mounted the bikes.

"First it's spinning, and now coffee! What will it be next week?" We both laughed.

As we sipped our lattes, I asked him, "Tell me about the pastry chef you're working with."

Christophe said, "Oh, I just say that, so people won't ask what I do anymore. People don't know what to say when you tell them you're studying with a pastry chef."

"So what do you really do?"

"I wrote a platform to manage a dental office completely online. We acquired 700 customers through trade shows. But the response time wasn't comparable to their Windows software. Every medical office uses a Windows desktop application. We had to compete with the relative speed of Windows. Our application just wasn't fast enough, so they all quit except two."

I could see immediately that he was an 80/20. But with his focus entirely on the software, he had missed a key element of reaching into his customer's mind.

"Man, I'm sorry I didn't know you then, Christophe, because I could have probably prevented you from losing those early subscribers."

"Hah! I hate you. How can you sit here and say that?" Even though he was joking, I could see he was upset.

As we chatted and sipped, I learned he had raised $2 million and spent it building the application and going to trade shows to acquire those customers. I shared what I saw.

"Christophe, what you missed was the opportunity to reset your customer's expectations. They were bound to their desk with Windows software. Sure, it was faster than running your application through a cloud server. But it would *never* free them from their desk. You had a chance to keep them as customers by binding them to your promise of freedom from their PC at the office."

During the uncomfortable silence that followed, I could taste that the coffee was getting cold. I asked, "What can you salvage from the ashes of the burned building?"

He instantly got my analogy and answered thoughtfully, "I'm really teased by the idea of just doing the schedule. It can be a lighter application and I don't see anyone doing this in the dental market."

"So what would that look like? How do you offer just a schedule online if the rest of the applications are on Windows, installed in the office PC?"

"Well, you put the schedule in the Cloud, and link it to the desktop. Then create an app for the medical staff and another mobile app for the dental clients."

I liked his idea. Suddenly, he seemed to have a lot of energy and inspiration to move on from the setback of losing all those customers. And it appeared that his application could scale to an even bigger mass market – not only in dental, but in any medical office or perhaps in the hospital market.

Rethink

Over the next several months, we did the spinning class every Saturday, and then we drank more coffee. We began meeting during the week, too. He had already begun programming the appointment solution. Since I don't write code, I began to think about branding, marketing, and how to get users to buy into the huge leverage they would experience by having access to their schedule online.

I invited my friend, Sam Horn, a genius branding expert to brainstorm a product name with us. She adeptly figured we could help her program a technical solution for a new product of her own. We agreed to trade services in a win-win process that she helped us see clearly.

After listening to everything we had dreamed up, she asked, "Have you heard of Ticketmaster?"

We both nodded.

"Well, this is AppointMaster!" she announced.

Her new branding cut through all of the clumsy names we had played with, using words like: *calendar, schedule, seat and chair.* AppointMaster conjured up a scheduling genie able to magically make appointments out of thin air. We instantly loved the idea and the brand!

We gained a few customers using email blasts, but the servers kept shutting us down for spam. If we were going to grow revenue, we needed a more reliable way to sign new customers.

After his prior unpleasant experience of raising and spending a lot of money without gaining an enduring customer base, Christophe was not interested in raising the money necessary to market our way to revenue. Yet, that is exactly what our competitors in the dental and chiropractic markets were doing. And there were competitors.

They had been going to trade shows to find individual medical practices to subscribe to their solutions, a process that took years and cost hundreds of thousands of dollars. I knew this from spending the past 30 years doing exactly that.

We needed to find another way to increase sales.

Innovate

I had just completed a multi-year effort focused on the wireless phone market. Our patents and primary research demonstrated that the technology could increase the data throughput of a cellular phone by three-to-five times. More importantly, it could reduce dropped calls using an "orthogonal wave propagation" (by beaming a spiral signal instead of an "up and down" sine wave pattern).

The big players had acquired customers by marketing their brand (think Sprint, T-Mobile, and AT&T). We needed a way to reach these customers without taking years and a pile of cash to do it. We decided to license our tech to the big brands for a fraction of their total subscription revenue. This could give us access to a trillion-dollar market by "bolting on" our solution to theirs. This way, we could gain direct access to their existing customer base without having to win them over one by one. I applied this thinking to our newly-minted AppointMaster brand.

Over the initial years, we kept our overhead low by working at home and I kept my day job selling software subscriptions in another market. We tried clever direct marketing, telemarketing, and finding sales reps to bring our new idea to their existing customers. Christophe created "integrations" to existing well-known practice management software. We hired their distributors to add our solution to their client installations.

I set a goal of reaching five percent market share within three years. This was totally arbitrary, but I kept thinking back to my conversation with Bill Hambrecht just a few years ago. We needed to reach a critical mass early in order to justify continuing. In short, we needed to iterate our failures – quickly – and then innovate or move on to ultimately reach our goal of "customers and revenue."

The dental and chiropractic markets were not growing quickly for us. There was enough embedded competition offering appointment scheduling solutions that were "good enough" that we could not break into their substantial base of users. We needed to find another market where competition was lower.

Fail Fast

During a November visit to Ohio, my friend Ralph invited me to join a ride with some fellow cyclists. It was so cold we each bumped fists through our gloved hands and spoke through balaclavas that were protecting our faces from the twenty-degree biting wind. So much for conversation, I thought!

But as we rolled out, one of the riders, a guy named Drake, told me he owned a veterinary software company. I tried to tell him about AppointMaster and finally realized it was futile speaking through so many layers. We agreed to meet later for coffee and a demo. The coffee was great, but we couldn't get an internet connection. We rescheduled. Twice. Finally, days later, he saw what we had.

"No one is doing this in the veterinary market. And if they did, it failed. I would know, because I've been in that market for five years and I know all the players."

"Can we put together an exclusive arrangement with your company?" I ventured. "We would integrate our solution into your practice management software."

"Hmm. That might work," he said, thoughtfully

Over the coming weeks, we made several trips to Ohio to meet with Drake and his team. Sure enough, we were able to get an exclusive with his company. I referred to this relationship over the next few years as our "Petrie dish" where we could experiment – and **Fail Fast** - with new ideas putting us in direct contact with their hospitals, veterinarians and pet parents across the country. This real-time experimentation enabled us to accelerate our learning, to continually rethink what was working – and not working – test innovations, rinse, and repeat. As a result, we got better faster.

Succeed

I repeated my imaginary mantra: "We want to achieve a five-percent market penetration in the next three years."

"I get it," Drake said, "but you won't get there with us because we're too small."

He knew the bigger players because they were each in competition with him for the same clients. His casual response to my mantra of "five-percent-in-three-years" was the first time that I felt it must be possible.

"Can you introduce us to the top companies in the vet space?"

"Yes, I can do that if you'll make it worth my while to introduce you to my competitors."

And we did. He received a small share of our company stock in exchange for introductions and ongoing guidance that ultimately helped us maximize the value of what we had created.

Among Drake's competitors, one company "had something already in the works," and a pilot "with about 500 hospitals." They declined to meet with us. Another had tried to implement something similar to what we had, but had failed. The largest provider of practice management software fell into the latter category.

And we were able to ink a deal with them to integrate our solution with their backend database structure.

We kept our "Petrie dish" laboratory at Drake's company so we could continuously try new innovations without exposing our "Fail Fast" strategy to too many clients. I consider this to be the "Rinse & Repeat" part of our Learning Wellth cycle. Over the next eight years, and with our corporate partner, we scaled subscriptions to 3,000 veterinary hospitals on three continents.

Instead of trying to be a new brand, we aligned with a large existing customer base for about half of the subscription revenue. Christophe's key innovation was to create an upstart application that would synchronize in real time with the incumbent Windows software. In this way, he created a win-win to allow medical staff and their clients each to do what was easiest for them.

By finding something as mundane as pet-appointment scheduling and working to create a better way to deliver it, we had achieved what Bill Hambrecht had guided me to do back in 2006.

Rinse & Repeat

Today, our cloud-based scheduling supports 100 million pets. Most of the same team is today working on an automated voice attendant to answer the phone for veterinarians. This turns out to be a major bottleneck for pet parents who want to schedule an appointment or report an emergency. While answering the phone seems to be an opportunity for staff to connect with clients, it turns out to be a real pain point. People don't want to wait on the phone to schedule or confirm routine appointments. The team employed a rinse & repeat strategy to extend their success in a proven market. Phone answering in a medical office is yet another mundane problem that can be addressed with an 80/20 solution.

Learning Wellth™ in Action

In today's rapidly changing world, staying ahead of the curve requires a mindset of continuous learning and adaptation, and a philosophy of embracing failure as a stepping stone to success. #learningwellth

Big Picture – Zoom Out

Learning Wellth highlights the importance of challenging the status quo and identifying outdated approaches to discover innovative solutions. Even seemingly mundane goods and services can become lucrative opportunities for innovation and disruption. This concept is particularly relevant in today's technology-driven economy where ephemeralization - the ability to deliver greater value at a fraction of the cost - is transforming industries.

Learn to adopt a *proactive* approach to learning and innovation. Asking insightful questions, trusting instincts, and actively participating in developing valuable ideas are crucial steps towards achieving Learning Wellth.

Tactics – Ideas to Action

To successfully implement the "Rethink – Fail Fast – Innovate – Succeed – Rinse & Repeat" process, these tactics will help you continually adapt and innovate to stay ahead in a rapidly changing world:

☐ **Identify Outdated Approaches:** Actively seek out areas where existing solutions fall short or fail to leverage new technologies or methodologies.

☐ **Look for Mundane Opportunities:** Don't overlook the potential for innovation in everyday goods and services. Often, the most significant opportunities lie in improving essential yet overlooked aspects of life.

☐ **Ask Insightful Questions:** Engage in conversations with a focus on understanding underlying problems and uncovering hidden opportunities. The key is to ask more questions than you answer.

☐ **Trust Your Instincts:** Don't be afraid to pursue ideas that resonate with you, even if they seem unconventional. Trusting your gut feeling can lead to unexpected breakthroughs.

☐ **Embrace "Fail Fast" Methodology:** Adopt a mindset of rapid experimentation, testing new ideas quickly and iterating based on results. View failure as an opportunity to learn and improve.

☐ **Build a "Petri Dish" Environment:** Seek out partnerships or collaborations that provide a safe space to test innovations and iterate quickly. This controlled environment allows for rapid learning and refinement without risking large-scale failures.

☐ **Rinse & Repeat:** Continuous improvement is essential for sustained success. Continuously analyze what works and what doesn't, adapt your approach, and repeat the process to achieve ongoing growth.

☐ **Seek Out Agile Partnerships:** Align with companies or individuals who embrace a culture of continuous learning and adaptation. These partnerships can significantly accelerate your learning curve and open up new opportunities for innovation.

Your Turn ✍

Do you see a way to use the "Rethink" process in your life?

What is the status quo that you want to rethink?

What would be the outcome of implementing this process... at work? at home? in your social or sports club?

How can you apply this to your relationships?

What action can you take now that will make you more resilient?

Chapter 4

Earning Wellth

"A big part of financial freedom is having your heart and mind free from worry about the what-ifs of life."

Suze Orman

In **Earning Wellth,** my wife and I hit a point in our lives where we needed to expand our understanding about money in order to create personal peace of mind and a mindset of abundance. We sought clarity with our financial advisors, who helped us align our different beliefs and strategies into shared goals as we approached retirement.

Two Kinds of Money

While on a Zoom meeting with my financial counselor and fellow cyclist, Ralph Antolino, I mentioned, "I'm having some difficulty explaining to Jill where our income comes from now that I'm retired."

Jill and I had made the shift from both of us earning a paycheck to a new phase in which we took distributions from our investment income.

With a smile, Ralph said, "Well, the simplest explanation is that there are two kinds of money: when *people* are working and when *money* is working. You have both."

"Wow, that's the best definition I've heard," and I shared this with Jill. It opened up a discussion for us about how "*money* working" feels different from "*people* working" when it comes to experiencing your emotions.

The monthly paycheck is so tangible when you are trading hours for dollars, that it tends to be a solid comfort. It's tangible; it feels like security, even though it isn't.

If you haven't experienced *money* working as your sole source of income, it can, at first, cause some anxiety as, generally, it means investments in stocks and bonds…and the market goes up and down. But, on the other hand, it offers long-term security knowing that your principal is protected in investments of minimal-risk dividend-paying stocks.

This kind of peace of mind is new to Jill and me and growing more real. It may be new to you as well. Or, you may be years from the "distribution" phase of your financial life.

To be honest, over my working career, it was great getting that pat on the back every two weeks when I was earning a paycheck – for 45 years. I *knew* where the money was coming from.

People Working

However, now that I'm retired and Jill is working part-time, we don't see the balances going up, except when we move money from our investment account to our checking accounts. But then it's like giving ourselves a payday. We are now what is called "distributors," managing our monthly accounts with quarterly transfers.

Money Working

Ralph and his colleagues introduced us to their Values and Goals questionnaire in their proprietary client survey, "The Ultravision System." Jill and I answered the questions separately and compared our answers to see where we were in and out of alignment.

"The challenge," Ralph offered, "is that 50% of our clients don't complete our survey. And without this crucial starting place, it's impossible to know how someone feels and what someone wants. We're not mind readers."

Financial Awareness and Security is Very Emotional

Fear of scarcity drives most disagreements between couples over money.

"It is the leading cause of divorce," declares NYU professor and best-selling author Scott Galloway. This fear runs so deep that only 35% of Americans are working with a financial adviser, revealed a Northwestern Mutual 2022 Planning & Progress Study.

Perhaps this is from a prejudice against getting help, concern at the expense of getting a financial advisor or a misplaced belief that you have to have money to get help with money. Or, even more likely, an emotional inclination to postpone what we perceive as unpleasant things we'd rather not face head-on.

Another Northwestern Mutual Study revealed stark differences in how Gen Z and millennials feel about financial uncertainty. These population sectors reported that, at least once a month, it:

- Makes them feel depressed – 36%
- Keeps them up at night – 34%

- Impacts their relationship with their spouse/partner – 28%
- Causes them to miss out on social events and opportunities – 28%
- Creates issues with friends or family (other than spouses/partners) – 26%
- Makes them physically ill – 24%
- Impacts their job performance – 24%

"That used to be me," I thought to myself.

The opportunity to get this right is gigantic. It is predicted that over $70 trillion will transfer from the baby boomer generation to GenX, Millennials, and GenZ over the next ten years.

I always think of a bit that comic Jeff Foxworthy did as the popular TV host of *Are You Smarter Than a 5th Grader?* It's on the difference between single money and married money and it goes something like this:

"Single money is great!" he says. "You buy anything you want whenever you want it.

"But married money? Oh, that's different. You put it in the middle of the living room floor and then circle around it like sharks. When new furniture arrives, or a boat shows up in the driveway, you both exclaim: 'What?!?! How'd that happen?'"

It's serious, but Foxworthy is a genius at getting us to laugh about it.

Author Galloway says it's an epic and worthy challenge "...to get clear about who is going to earn the money, and how it gets spent between couples."

I am blessed in so many ways, but especially with a smart and loving wife. When I was coming to the end of my working career, I was struggling with the notion that I had not yet achieved my goals.

One morning, as I was lamenting over this, Jill wisely told me, "John, you are enough. You did enough. You have enough. We have enough."

Deep within my soul, I knew she was right. After working for four decades without a real plan for retirement, I was running on pure adrenaline and a fear that I would *never* have enough.

Does that feel familiar?

Ralph had us take the Values and Goals questionnaire, something we had delayed, just like so many people. We answered the survey questions separately, but at the same time. And we shared our answers with each other before sharing them with our advisor in Ralph's firm.

They revealed something about our different priorities that made sense and was exactly the non-emotional information that we needed in order to reach a compromise: Jill's priority when it came to investments was less risk and more security; mine was high-returning risk.

That gave us something to talk about.

Understanding Jill's concern that we could lose money, I agreed to seek more moderate risks; as for Jill, she agreed to trust me and this process.

Then Jill and I created a commitment letter to each other and Ralph's firm based on our new understanding.

This financial map provided us with guide points to help us navigate the coming years. And we were able to clearly see how different, yet valid, our priorities were, and thus know for the first time that it was important that we satisfy both of us. This process was vital in helping us understand the path we were on − together.

Once we took the survey, we regretted not doing it sooner!

The unique and important element in how the survey questions are framed helped us get to the heart of our fears, hopes and opportunities. This process helped us go beyond the simple math of financial performance. Antolino Associates has developed a sophisticated "Math Model" that helps project our financial security based on market performance with our portfolio of investments.

In addition to this, they helped us dive into the "why" behind our goals, fears and opportunities. This unique and important element of their service helps us say "no" to things that don't fit with our plans. When you understand your "why," it empowers you to stick to your financial plan when opportunities come up that are not in alignment.

Here are some of the prompts:

- "In three years, as you look back on your personal and professional life, you will feel happy about your progress if..."

Our answers were quite different and revealed to us where we felt uneasy or confident.

- "What is important about money to you?"

We were in close alignment with each other around meeting needs for housing and healthcare.

- "What are your three-year dangers, opportunities and strengths?"

These answers revealed so much about unspoken uncertainties and fears! It also encouraged us to brainstorm about opportunities to get better organized, such as creating a binder with our insurance policies and physical assets.

We had to set down our phones and to really think about things that we had not ever considered "in one picture frame." Our new view of how we each felt on these subjects brought us relief.

And while our answers differed, we learned that we shared long-term goals. It gave us a new sense of togetherness; we now had authentic answers to tough questions.

Sitting side by side with Jill on a Zoom call with our advisor, my relief was palpable looking at the projections. I could feel the tension in my jaw relax.

In Financial Planning 101, you learn that the sooner you start to save, the better. Take a look at the number one best-selling personal finance book of all time by Robert Kiyosaki called *Rich Dad, Poor Dad*. In it, Kiyosaki describes the difference in financial philosophies between his real (poor) dad and his friend's (rich) dad. The poor dad had been taught to work hard, bank a paycheck, buy a house and spend his life paying off the mortgage. The rich dad believed in renting a house, thus freeing up his money for investments that would make him more money than any one job.

I wanted to understand the power of leverage, when money invested earns more money without working a job to get it. I discovered from Bill Hambrecht that if you don't have capital, you can use your intellect and efforts ("sweat equity") to gain an interest in a business. I have been doing that ever since.

Ralph taught me about the extraordinary power of compound interest, where it creates interest *on* interest, as well as on principal. It is so powerful that it's worth restating. Let's look at a possible scenario of two people who invest the same $2,400/year. The first starts at age 21, and stops at age 30. The second starts investing at age 30 and continues to age 67. The total invested by each is $21,600 by the first one, and $88,800 by the second one. At an annual rate of return of 11%, the first one has $2.1 million at age 67. The second one has $1.2 million.

The amount is $900,000 less for the second person. The big picture is that saving and investing earlier has a substantial impact due to the power of compound interest.

Our advisor introduced us to two more tools on our path. These are Accounts and Buffers.

The ABC "Buckets" of Money

A = Accounts. Are your spendable balances sufficient to pay *three* months of bills? Do you have credit card debt? That's the opposite of this goal, so start there. Using only a debit card while you pay off debt transforms into the helpful practice of "you can't spend it if you don't have it."

B = Buffer. Plan to set aside *six* months of funds for emergencies or large unplanned expenses.

C = Compounding. Get some money market accounts or annuities, so that you have "money working" to earn more money based on principles of risk and reward. Make sure any credit cards you have give you rewards that go toward your bill or gift cards; it's free money.

This clarity brought us peace of mind, a kind of financial emotional wellness that we call **Earning Wellth.**

It's Never Too Early or Late to Learn About Money

Ralph told me that when he was 11 years old, his mother would sit at the kitchen table wringing her hands, proclaiming "We don't have enough money to pay the bills! I can't balance the checkbook!"

Although their family never missed a meal, his mother, born during the Great Depression, always worried about money. Ralph vividly remembered her anxious looks and worrisome comments.

As a little kid he wanted to help his mother. So he cautiously went to the table and asked her what was wrong. She threw the bank statement at him and repeated again how they were out of money.

This time he decided to see if he could help her. He carefully read the bank statement and started to follow the step-by-step instructions on the back of the form on how to balance the checkbook.

After a little time, he was able to show her that they did have enough money after all! This brought a big smile to her face and made him feel important and valuable. It was a skill she didn't have, and he realized for the first time that she didn't have the capacity to gain that skill. Knowing her little boy could help her made them both incredibly happy.

It also burned into his psyche that he needed to learn about this money thing.

Emotional Deposits and Withdrawals

What Ralph learned was that there is great emotional value in helping others solve problems that they are not well-equipped to solve. Some learn that it is just not their strength or not their inclination, or perhaps something that they were never taught to do.

We each have our strengths and weaknesses. Forcing results in areas in which we are uneducated or insecure produces frustrations and anxieties, depleting our **Emotional Bank Accounts** and creating stress.

About fifteen years ago, I confronted the reality that I am a poor bookkeeper. So, I hired a bookkeeping service and gave them access to my bank accounts. Then I hired a CPA and gave him access to my books. These two helped me run my life like the early-stage businesses I was helping to launch. Next, I retained a lawyer to work with me on my early-stage ventures.

This enabled me to have the perspective of three advisers on-demand.

It came with a nominal cost, but it freed me up to focus on creative thinking and problem-solving. The critical path for an early stage enterprise is to move from their big idea to a product, and then to attracting customers to generate revenue. This is the holy grail of early-stage enterprise. If you can get from the idea phase to customers and recurring revenue, then your new company is very likely to survive the first three years when 50% of new businesses fail.

Building relationships with those who have strengths in the areas where we are weak is a key to building a growing **Emotional Wellth Account**. When you have a balance, you can make a withdrawal. If not, you run a deficit or risk being bankrupt in that **Emotional Account**. This is how we first experience this concept.

Ralph describes his mother as a professional worrier, by virtue of being raised in poverty, and by her own nature and lack of training. He observed that she would create all sorts of things to worry about. As long as she was "unable" to balance the checkbook, she could worry about not having enough money. She had an emotional deficit in the area of self-confidence about money. There was enough money to meet their needs, but her perception was framed by the relative scarcity she experienced in her childhood that resulted in a lifelong pattern of want.

Observing his mother's monthly outbursts about money taught Ralph that patience, confidence in yourself, and problem-solving skills can go a long way toward building a surplus in your **Earning Wellth Account**. By making monetary deposits you prepare for an inevitable crisis or withdrawal. Similarly, you gain poise for how to navigate these events.

For example, Ralph and I were discussing a project we were both interested in promoting. As we looked at options for attending events and marketing the product, he said something I'll never forget:

"We can do anything, but we can't do everything."

That spoke to the heart of what happens when your ABC's are working as designed and struck me in its simplicity, its wisdom and its balance. ABC planning enables your ability to choose wisely and in harmony with your goals and values.

"Another way to think about ABC planning," grinned Ralph, "is that it allows you to have enough money available to feel authentically secure, so that what you do spend, you can spend without remorse."

And who wants a life filtered through remorse?

Earning Wellth™ in Action

Two Kinds of Money – when "**you** are working," and when "**money** is working," you can create personal peace of mind and a whole new way of being in a position of plenty. #earningwellth

Big Picture – Zoom Out

Transitioning from a regular paycheck to relying on investments for income can be a challenging and emotional experience. Understanding the difference between "*people* working" (earning a paycheck) and "*money* working" (earning through investments) can bring clarity and peace of mind in retirement. This framework helps individuals navigate the emotional and practical aspects of managing finances post-retirement. **Earning Wellth** should inspire readers to embrace both kinds of money and understand the importance of financial planning for long-term security and emotional well-being.

The bigger idea here is the necessity of financial literacy, strategic planning and emotional alignment when transitioning into retirement or any phase where investment income becomes a primary source. It's about recognizing that financial security involves both tangible assets and intangible peace of mind.

By understanding and implementing the principles of financial planning, individuals can transform their anxiety about money into a structured and positive approach toward their financial future. The narrative underscores the interconnectedness of financial wellbeing and emotional health, suggesting that **Earning Wellth** is a harmonious balance of both.

Tactics – Ideas to Action

By following these tactics, individuals can achieve a balanced approach to financial planning that supports both their emotional and financial well-being. This holistic strategy ensures long-term security and peace of mind, enabling a more fulfilling life in retirement and beyond.

Understand the Two Kinds of Money:

- ☐ *People* **Working:** Income derived from active work, like a salary or wages.
- ☐ *Money* **Working:** Income derived from investments, savings and other passive sources.
- ☐ Know which phase you are in and plan accordingly.

Develop a Financial Plan:

- ☐ Engage with a financial advisor to create a comprehensive financial plan that includes income sources, expenses and investment strategies.
- ☐ Use tools like surveys to align financial goals and values between partners.

Build a Buffer for Peace of Mind:

- ☐ Maintain account balances sufficient to cover three months of expenses.
- ☐ Have a buffer of six months worth of funds for emergencies or significant planned expenses.

Leverage the Power of Compounding:

☐ Start saving early to take advantage of compound interest.

☐ Understand that delaying savings can significantly impact long-term financial outcomes.

Emotional and Financial Alignment:

☐ Use "values and goals" surveys to ensure emotional and financial alignment within families or between partners.

☐ Discuss financial priorities openly to reduce anxiety and ensure mutual understanding.

Create a Commitment Letter:

☐ Draft a financial commitment letter outlining shared goals, fears, strengths, and opportunities.

☐ Use this document as a guide to navigate financial decisions together.

Educate Yourself and Your Family:

☐ Read foundational personal finance books like *Rich Dad, Poor Dad* to build financial literacy.

☐ Teach younger generations the value of money and the principles of saving and investing.

Strategic Spending and Saving:

☐ Plan your spending to align with financial goals and values, ensuring you can spend without remorse.

☐ Prioritize investments in a way that supports long-term financial health and well-being.

Resources

The UltraVision System®[1] – The ABC's of Money

In the book *Pinocchio*, Jiminy Cricket once exclaimed that "a conscience is that still, small voice that people won't listen to…"

Think of "Jiminy Cricket" as a reminder to set a deadline for yourself to create an investment and financial security system. Write it in your calendar and stop saying "I really should…"

And remember the power of compounding: Start early, or start later, but *start* because the cost of waiting is high!

---

[1] https://www.antolino.com/ultravision-system

Your Turn ✍

How do you – or will you – feel about money ...today?

...three years from now?

...in a generation?

What would help you feel safe in your own **ABC** accounts?

What's the next step you want to take toward leaving a financial legacy for your family?

What did your parents model for you about money?

Are you in a deficit or a positive Earning Wellth balance?

Chapter 5
Giving Wellth

"Your perceived failure can become the catalyst for profound reinvention."

Conan O'Brien

D o you donate your time or money to a favorite charity? Doing so is setting in motion our passion to make a difference, thus becoming the ultimate act of compassion. It puts us in the active mode of gratitude and grows resilience in ourselves and those we aid. But what if that nonprofit is shrinking, soon to disappear? In **Giving Wellth**, I focus on improving nonprofits' structure and operations so they can deliver on their mission. In this story, I focus on the importance of overhead in the success of a nonprofit and propose some ways to make charitable giving more sustainable. **Charitable donations leverage billions each year that help us build and sustain resilience as a nation.**

Sustainable Charity

Giving makes our heart grow, and then, "poof!" the organization we gave to runs out of money! How can we get better at this?

We are living in an *Age of Connection.* It is from this strong sense of connection that we can express our caring. The #1 economy on earth also has the biggest heart: We give nearly $500 billion to charities each year. However, we think that cause-driven giving will magically support itself. Unfortunately, because most charities don't think or behave like a *for*-profit business, they are prone to falling short.

A chance introduction at a nonprofit conference led to a refreshing new view of this old paradigm. I was introduced to an inventor who applied creative problem-solving to create improved outcomes for pregnant mothers and babies.

Coming from a strong business background, I had a low regard for nonprofits. The giving is great, but they never seem to be around in a year.

My earliest experience was of my bicycle-racing team, which was always running out of money. Later I witnessed my father's nonprofit — from our kitchen table — paying conference deposits on his personal credit card, hoping that attendance will pay it off. Eventually, he put a second mortgage on his home to support the mission.

His nonprofit seemed to always be running out of money.

Nonprofits must learn that the term "nonprofit" is a tax status with the IRS and not a revenue prediction! And they must learn the importance of overhead being met when creating revenue for their cause. Any business must hire and invest in people, marketing, and management infrastructure if they want to be around another year.

Nonprofits, like any for-profit business, need products and customers. But the bottom line, sadly, is that if you don't have consistent funding sources to create the overhead you will need for success, you will eventually have learned a hard lesson at the expense of your passionate goals.

My father was an early leader and board member of the Association for Prenatal and Perinatal Psychology and Health (APPPAH), which turned 40 in 2023 and is still going strong. APPPAH focuses the importance of babies life in the womb and the impact this experience has on the rest of their life. In 1979, my father and APPPAH founder, Dr. Tom Verny, had begun corresponding regularly. He finally met up with Dr. Verny in the Green Room on *The Merv Griffin Show*, of all places. Dr. Verny had written an international bestselling book, *The Secret Life of the Unborn Child*, published in 1982 and Merv Griffin had invited him to tell the TV world all about the interesting topic of life in the womb.

As early as 1974, my father had begun collecting forgotten memories of birth in his counseling practice. I was a teenager then, learning to type in high school. To help me practice, Dad gave me the job of typing the transcripts of his counseling sessions. When I typed the first birth memory, he explained to me that no one would believe these theories!

"Modern psychology – and Freud – hold that humans are either cognitive or behavioral, but it does not embrace the existence of a soul," he explained. "No one in modern psychology will believe what my clients are saying about their own births, because they are reporting experiences that happened to them *before* the brain and language are formed. These experiences require the presence of a soul before the physical body is ready for its life after birth."

He set out to demonstrate the reliability of these memories. He studied parent-child pairs who had never discussed the child's birth. Amazingly, the research revealed as many as 19 dovetails between the parent's experience and the child's. You can read about the findings in his 1988 book *Babies Remember Birth.*

He also created a website (a new thing at the time) and branded it "Birth Psychology." The site BirthPsychology.com receives thousands of unique visits every day from over one hundred countries. And so began my father's global journey to share this news with the world.

Late in 2013, I was recovering from the bad accident you will read more about in Chapter Seven. I was still on crutches in mid-December when my phone rang. It was Sandra, the new President of APPPAH, who introduced herself and promptly asked me to join the Board of Directors. I said "No, thank you," without thinking twice.

"I love the organization's mission," I explained, "but I disagree fundamentally with how they go to market. Plus, I'm not a psychologist or a birth professional. In any event, I don't think I qualify."

"Well," she said, "I am sitting with your father at his kitchen table and he says APPPAH needs someone with your business skills." She went on to say he had shared with her my passion for early stage enterprise and creating sales in companies that have hit a revenue plateau.

("Wow," I thought, "now I am feeling cornered – and by my own father!")

"Well, that changes things a bit," I sighed, wishing to get *off* the phone. "Why don't you send me the application and I'll fill it out."

As I had said, I did not think I would qualify. Quietly, I hoped that I wouldn't. With my significant injuries, I was not looking for a new project – I was just trying to survive!

Well, I qualified.

My experience of nonprofits was influenced strongly by my father's nonprofit in birth psychology. While my career centered on sales and strategic skills, he focused on counseling and research. How could we resolve these two personal trajectories to achieve a greater good?

I asked myself, why was I so hesitant to give? What could help me feel better about my giving? In effect, what was holding me back from helping my father?

The more I thought about it, the more I realized that the organization didn't have the mindset or organizational structure to sustain itself financially. Could this be a wider concern for nonprofits in general?

When I joined the **APPPAH** board in April 2014, they put me in charge of the marketing committee to fill an empty "seat" in that function. This was not a good match for my strategic planning and operational skills. What's more, they had only $15,000 in the bank and could not meet payroll for their Executive Director. They needed to urgently generate more revenue. Sadly, as many people realize when they get involved with a nonprofit, it looked like I was jumping onto a sinking ship.

I like working on complex problems for which others have not found a solution. I've learned to bring convergent thinking and a deep pool of relationships to create practical solutions, focused on a high probability of success. I attended a board retreat in January that year to observe how things were working out, and I brought one of my business plans that I had been working on for about five years. When they saw it, they remarked "I wish you could write a business plan for APPPAH."

I replied, "I would love to if I only knew what to write. I don't see a sustainable business model here."

Another Princeton friend, Bill, came from a for-profit career in business. When he transitioned into a nonprofit for deaf children, he realized they could only afford a Board of Volunteers. Thinking of his situation, it was clear to me that APPPAH was stuck in a mindset that would enable them to only sustain a 100% volunteer organization.

I told the board, "You need something to drive repeat revenue. It could be certification and professional fees, or some other way to provide cash flow from an increasing number of members. And you need overhead to generate revenue, or else you begin to shrink and you lose the ability to generate new ideas and act on them. It looks like you're trying to reduce overhead to meet ever-lower revenue expectations. This is the opposite of a successful business model."

Fast forward ten years. Stephen Gyllenhaal produced a documentary called **Uncharitable**, the story about how misperceptions in the nonprofit world can lead to disastrous outcomes. Gyllenhaal reflects on the "high price of low overhead" that brought down the remarkably successful Wounded Warrior Project (WWP). At its peak, WWP chalked up three times the overhead costs of nonprofits their size. Although criticized for that, their expanded overhead proceeded to deliver six times the charitable contribution of comparable organizations. The documentary is about Dan

Pallotta's TED talk, seen over five million times, which demonstrates that *overhead* can actually be good.

I wish I had been able to elaborate to the board in 2014 what Dan Pallotta told us nine years later in 2023 in this groundbreaking movie. From my observation over many years, watching my father's frustrated participation, I believed APPPAH was sitting on the outside of the $50 billion hospital birth market – and ignoring it, the 800-pound gorilla in the room.

The collected wisdom at the time was that hospital birth practices were creating separation between mother and baby when their research showed mom and baby needed to be together. Directly or indirectly, through research, APPPAH and its allies blamed hospitals for causing trauma in newborns with their standardized procedures of holding them upside down, spanking, cutting foreskin of boys, piercing their skin, using chemicals without permission or anesthesia, or leaving them to cry alone.

Various discoveries, made through the use of psychoanalysis and neuroscientific research, revealed that a mother and baby should have skin-to-skin contact immediately following the birth. Babies need to be intimately close to the person who carried and fed them during their first nine months in utero. It is enough of an effort to be born!

I spent the next two years looking for a way to connect the APPPAH mission of research and education to a consistent revenue stream. Their most significant asset was a 30-year publication of peer-reviewed research in the professional Journal of Prenatal and Perinatal Psychology and Health (JOPPPAH). This is the only resource in the world of articles on the psychological aspects of birth and before.

Unfortunately, the Journal had been poorly monetized, selling only through university and allied organization subscriptions.

A second possibility for sustained revenue was to create upward mobility among its membership ranks. Perhaps this could be achieved by connecting birth psychologists to labor and delivery hospitals or by promoting paid training of midwives and doulas in prenatal and perinatal psychology. The goal would be to create professional certification approved by hospital maternity departments (and their third- party review agencies). This would elevate APPPAH's professionals, and create ongoing training revenue.

To build and offer certification in birth psychology would mean that birth professionals all over the world could receive training in how to prevent early life trauma. In turn, they could leverage their career in the new field of birth psychology. The APPPAH Director of Education was working on such a program – for Prenatal and Perinatal Educators. This certification training could encompass life in utero as well as during and immediately following birth.

A third possibility was under discussion to begin a regional conference in the intervening years between the international conferences. This could build revenue by increasing membership in specific regions around each conference and could attract more local sponsors. By moving a regional conference around the country it would serve to build membership and expand the universe of sponsors associated with our nonprofit.

I had a lot of research to do if we were going to turn things around.

After deep immersion in this material for two years, I created a business plan for APPPAH. The plan focus was to empower and train **APPPAH** professional members to conduct training of labor and delivery medical personnel in hospitals. My "Places of Birth" business proposed to retrain everyone who touches a newborn baby or supports the mother and father during preconception, gestation, labor, birth and postpartum.

The primary goal was to create upward mobility within **APPPAH** for its members to see economic value from investing in continuing education and professional certification. It was designed to create recurring revenue for **APPPAH** from the $50 billion U.S. market for hospital maternity.

A funny thing happened along the way. After drafting the business plan in 2016, I was asked to speak about it at the first **APPPAH** regional conference in Seattle. The conference was held on the campus of Bastyr University – a progressive health practitioner school north of the city. This conference became the proof case that a regional conference could increase membership and revenue.

I prepared a brief set of slides to tell the story of our plan to serve Practitioners, Parents, and Places of Birth. I dubbed the plan "Three P's in a Pod," in a cute analogy of conceptual triplets in-utero. Since my father was a well-known thought leader in birth psychology, I began my talk by saying: "I love the mission of **APPPAH**. Besides being born into the right household, at home we playfully say *the APPPAH didn't fall far from the tree.*" People laughed and I felt reassured that my participation on this turn-around journey was welcomed.

A friend on the board, a doula named Barb, suggested I introduce myself to a man who was new to **APPPAH**. She suggested that he may be able to contribute to the organization. He was standing nearby in the lobby, so I walked up and welcomed him to the conference. He introduced himself as Dick Sass.

"How did you come to find us here at Bastyr?"

"Steven Bezruchka, a professor at "U Dub," told me I should come."

"And how did he know about us?"

"He knows one of your board members who's a doula. She goes by the name "DoulaDecker," he grinned.

"Yes! I know her. That's wonderful. What does Steven do?"

Dick answered without hesitation. "Population studies at the University of Washington. He authored a paper that got my attention called "Early Life or Early Death," based on the science and statistics of Developmental Origins of Health and Disease, known as DOHaD."

"I didn't know that was a science."

"Yes, it is, and it can change how we live or die in the coming generations."

"Wow, how did you become interested in that?"

"I have an adopted son whose life was changed," he said, leaning into the cocktail table where we were standing, "for the worse, by fetal alcohol syndrome. This led to a range of dysfunctions in his teenage and young adult life. And, well, ultimately, it led to drug abuse and prison."

"That's a sad story, Dick. I'm so sorry to hear about all the challenges with your son. How does that connect you to being here today?"

Dick told me a story about his father's copper wire distribution business in the Midwest.

"After finding success in the railroad business, I discovered there was demand for many other wire types and materials. So I formed a new company to sell 'noble' wires into the healthcare market, named *noble* because they can live inside the body without being rejected. That's Platinum, silver, and gold."

I immediately liked that he saw a new market and set up a company to capitalize on it. "This is my kind of guy!" I thought as I listened to more of his story.

"One thing led to another, and I got a patent for an implantable CGM device. That's a Continuous Glucose Monitor. It's used to help diabetics continuously track their blood sugar without having to stick their finger every 10 minutes."

"Oh, wow. That must be a huge market," I whistled. "My wife of 16 years is a Type 1 juvenile diabetic. She has to test her blood twice a day to decide how much insulin to add to her shot. When we were pregnant, she had to have a test every three hours. I helped stick her toes because her fingers became so sore. I didn't know that it was now possible to monitor blood sugar continuously under the skin! That's a huge breakthrough. Thank you!"

"Yes, there are 40 million diabetics in the U.S. today. If we can help moms have a better pregnancy, and lower diabetes in the next generations, this can translate into reduced healthcare costs in the future. And bigger, healthier babies can translate into a bigger, healthier economy."

I pondered that for a moment. Even a fraction of that market for CGM's could be worth a fortune! I remembered then that "DoulaDecker" had mentioned that Dick might be interested in contributing to APPPAH. We were going to have that conversation right now. I cut to the chase: "Dick, have you considered making a significant gift to APPPAH?"

"I would love to," he replied instantly, much to my surprise and relief, "but the timing isn't right for me at the moment." And then he continued as though he had already decided what to say next.

"However, I would consider something else that may be of interest to you and APPPAH. I'm willing to license access to your 30-years of peer-reviewed professional research and articles of JOPPPAH."

This, too, took me by surprise. No one had ever come along who saw monetary value in JOPPPAH. I could see that he had thought through his request. That was just the type of recurring revenue APPPAH needed to be sustainable, to build overhead to create business success. We needed people to address the mass maternity market in a meaningful way.

"How would that work?" I asked.

"I'm working on an avatar that could be a virtual coach for a pregnant woman. It would be HIPPA-compliant and become a trusted resource of advice about exercise, stress relief and nutrition during pregnancy. We need to 'inform' the avatar with all the birth psychology that has ever been studied, written and presented in your professional Journal."

I was astonished by his project, and I didn't want to lose any momentum in our conversation. "How much does an avatar cost?"

"Turns out it's a *lot*. But when you factor the cost to develop it over four million births each year, it could be as little as $2/day to a pregnant woman. The best program in the U.S. today is by the Nurse-Family Partnership. It's a great program that's really getting results. But it costs thousands of dollars per family, so it can't be scaled to the mass market for pregnancy and postpartum coaching."

I was beginning to fall into the groove on his idea. "What would the license fees be for ongoing access to the Journal content?"

"I can offer a 2% royalty payment for a non-exclusive global license of all past, present, and future research reported in JOPPPAH. We would use the database to inform the avatar in all respects of pre- and perinatal health to influence DOHaD."

This took a moment to sink in as I performed a back-of-the-envelope calculation on four million births per year times $2/day/mom. That was a *substantial* number.

I smiled. "Alright. Let's work together to make this happen."

We shook hands again and there began one of my most cherished friendships and a business relationship that has had a positive impact on pregnant women and their babies – *and* on the rest of my career. Dick and I have since stayed in each other's homes in Oregon and Virginia and crisscrossed the country on behalf of this cause.

A year later, as CFO of APPPAH, I had the pleasure to announce that we had signed an agreement on May 1st of 2017 (the third anniversary of my father's passing) for a 2% royalty "in perpetuity" from subscriptions to the health- coach avatar.

I have since fulfilled my board duties and moved back into the private sector. Here are my take-aways from my nonprofit experience:

- Think like a for-profit business that has special tax status.
- Find and build recurring revenue for your organization.
- Write job descriptions for every position.
- Perform "hiring" interviews like the private sector.
- See overhead as good and necessary to get more contributions.
- Build four-deep leadership in every board function. If you have a working board, name a chairperson, assistant chair, secretary, and creative development

person. This provides better succession planning to prevent burnout.

- Recruit a philanthropic board to secure your financial needs.
- Develop and publish a five-year strategic plan.

If you are considering getting involved with a charity, or even just donating to it, be sure and look for the points above and how many years the nonprofit has been going, as well as their results.

If you've been asked to join a board of directors and these things aren't in place, perhaps you can start discussions about longevity that make these points. If people aren't receptive, you might consider a different organization in which to invest your time and money, because you want to be involved with one that comes from a compassionate heart, but works with a business-minded brain.

Giving Wellth™ in Action

By giving back, we can move humankind forward and grow our own hearts. In order for nonprofits to succeed, they need a "for-profit" mindset that will enable them to achieve their long-term mission. Dick Sass had a life experience that led him to create a foundation to improve maternal health. He could have cashed out on his patents but instead is harnessing leading-edge epigenetic research to help moms "build a better baby." His strong business skills and a passionate focus is a win-win – by design. #givingwellth

Big Picture – Zoom Out

Giving to charity is a powerful way to make positive impacts on society, but many nonprofits struggle to maintain financial stability. **Giving Wellth** emphasizes the importance of strategic contributions that not only aid the cause but also support the sustainability and growth of the organization. By understanding the need for proper overhead and structured business practices, we can help charities thrive and achieve their missions more effectively. This section aims to inspire readers to approach charitable giving with a strategic mindset, ensuring their contributions lead to lasting and meaningful change.

The bigger idea here revolves around reimagining how nonprofits operate by incorporating sound business principles. The story illustrates that nonprofits, despite their altruistic goals, need to function with the same strategic rigor as for-profit businesses to avoid financial pitfalls and achieve long-term success. This involves understanding the critical role of overhead, developing sustainable revenue streams, and ensuring robust operational practices. The narrative underscores that effective philanthropy isn't just about giving generously; it's about giving wisely to foster resilient organizations capable of making a sustained impact.

Tactics – Ideas to Action

By adopting these tactics, nonprofits can transform themselves into resilient organizations capable of sustained impact, ensuring that the generous contributions they receive are put to the best possible use for lasting change.

By adopting these tactics you can make sure your contributions are worthy.

Embrace Overhead as Essential

☐ Recognize that overhead costs like salaries, marketing and infrastructure are necessary for the effective operation of a nonprofit.

☐ Advocate for overhead expenses in your donations, understanding that they contribute to the organization's ability to deliver on its mission.

Develop Sustainable Revenue Streams:

☐ Identify and cultivate consistent funding sources such as membership fees, certifications or licensing agreements.

☐ Look for opportunities to monetize valuable assets, like research publications or specialized training programs.

Implement Business Practices:

☐ Treat the nonprofit like a for-profit business with detailed job descriptions, structured hiring processes and performance evaluations.

☐ Develop a five-year strategic plan outlining clear goals and steps to achieve financial and operational stability.

Build a Robust Organizational Structure:

- ☐ Ensure that the board of directors includes members with diverse skills and experiences, particularly in business and finance.
- ☐ Create "four-deep" leadership within committee structures to ensure continuity and prevent burnout.

Engage in Strategic Philanthropy:

- ☐ Encourage strategic contributions that support both immediate needs and long-term sustainability.
- ☐ Engage donors and stakeholders in understanding the importance of investing in the nonprofit's infrastructure.

Foster Partnerships and Collaborations:

- ☐ Build relationships with individuals and organizations that can provide expertise, funding, or other resources.
- ☐ Consider licensing agreements or partnerships that can create recurring revenue and expand the nonprofit's impact.

Focus on Impact and Accountability:

- ☐ Develop metrics to evaluate the effectiveness of programs and initiatives.
- ☐ Communicate transparently with stakeholders about how funds are used and the impact they have.

Create Upward Mobility Opportunities:

- ☐ Offer professional development and certification programs to enhance the skills of those within the organization and broader community.
- ☐ Invest in the growth and development of staff and volunteers to foster loyalty and expertise.

Your Turn

Have you contributed to a charity or cause?

What motivated you most to participate?

Describe ways you experienced volunteer burnout.

How did you feel about reaching your goal?

How could you apply these tactics to your charitable
investments to improve their sustainability?

Chapter 6
Love Wellth

"Someday is not a day in the week."

Sam Horn

"Love recognizes no barriers. It jumps hurdles, leaps fences, penetrates walls to arrive at its destination full of hope."

Maya Angelou

Love **Wellth** emphasizes the significance of nurturing relationships through consistent, dedicated interactions. It underscores that maintaining strong connections, especially with family, requires conscious effort and scheduled time for meaningful engagement. It highlights that even amidst busy schedules and life's demands, prioritizing quality time with loved ones can lead to stronger bonds and more fulfilling relationships.

In this chapter I share how I risked losing touch with my only son as we both dove deeper and deeper into our busy lives. I show how we saved our relationship and grew close again.

8 AM Coffee with Chris

When my son Chris entered Law School, we had lived in the same city for about five years. This was the first time we had lived in the same city since he was ten years old because I divorced from his mom and had moved to a different state.

After so many years of visiting each other every other weekend during his teen years, and then quarterly college visits, I felt a bit detached. I loved my son and I knew he loved me. But relationships need nurturing or they thin out. I knew me, and I knew his capacity to fully immerse himself in something, just like I do. We spoke on the phone frequently, but I could feel the separation looming between my work and his new commitment to study law.

Here is an example of his ability to dive deeply into something new with intense focus. When Chris was ten, I bought him a Takamine acoustic guitar. The following week he bought a colorful electric guitar for $10 at a yard sale. He continued to play both.

He practiced, asked for lessons, practiced more, asked for longer lessons, joined the jazz band at school, practiced more, joined a garage band, and then wanted to train with a top guitar teacher in New York City. He created a demo CD and applied to the Berklee College of Music in Boston for their summer Guitar Camp. They invited Chris to attend, and he did!

At age 14 he got on a train to Boston to attend the camp. He played so well, they asked him to return to help out the next summer. He went on to play lead guitar in the #1 new band on the east coast, as rated by Fading Signal, a popular crowdsourced ranking in those days. I was so proud of him!

As the fall semester at Georgetown began, I immediately started to hear less and less from him. I was rowing every

Friday morning on the Potomac. We would start in a shroud of darkness under the Key Bridge, and finish as the sun came up through its arches by 7 AM. Then I would shower and head to DC to see my clients.

I felt especially fortunate to have this weekly routine. Chris and his girlfriend lived just 10 minutes from the boathouse. I was usually ready for a coffee by eight o'clock. I had an idea.

I called Chris. "Listen, I don't want to lose touch with you over the next three years because you'll be so busy with law school."

"Yeah," he said, "it's already mounting up with my job during the day and classes at night. And I'm in Section Three, a group that also reads the philosophy of law along with the black letter law and torts."

"Would you consider giving me 30 minutes each Friday," I asked carefully, "to share a cup of coffee? My boathouse is just 10 minutes from your apartment."

There was a longish pause on the line. I imagined he was quickly calculating what he could do with 26 hours a year! But to my pleasure, he said "Yes," and then, "How about if we meet this Friday at the coffee bar inside the law school across the hall from the library?"

So, it was set. And this began a wonderful journey together that gave me a window into my son and his experience of this intense Section Three path he had chosen.

During that first year we met at a table in the hallway across from the coffee bar. Some days, I wasn't completely sure I had his attention as he hefted a bag of thick books. And at 8:29 AM, he would give me a hug and disappear into the library. As I watched him go, week after week, I was thankful that we had carved out this time to be together.

There are so many things I could tell you about what I saw through his lens over the fall and winter that first year of law school. In short bursts, we plunged into Hobbes, Hegel, Kant, Plato and Socrates. We wrestled together through theories of all the Laws: Natural, Positive, Marxist and Realist. We had spirited discussions about the relationship between law and morality, using examples from his textbooks.

The coffee was always hot during these brief times together, and I only had two parking tickets that first year when our conversations went longer. After the fall, the river iced over and without my rowing excuse, I found a place to sit at the Starbucks next to the law school to wait out the rush hour.

One morning, at 7 AM, by surprise, Chris found me at my hangout. We sat there through his feta cheese and spinach breakfast. Until then, the time limit on our half-hour had been inviolate, and now we were pushing 45 minutes!

Through him I had been vicariously swimming in his state of intense concentration as he breathed in, pulled another strong stroke, breathed out, week in and week out. I knew well by now that the Law Library opened at 7 AM. I even became able to feel his urgency to hit the books, like waves of heat from the sun.

"I remember you telling me how you met your new friend Brad on the first day of class: You set down your water bottle next to his in a lecture you both were taking and you both hit it off. How's that going?"

"Brad is a second-year full-time student. I'm in the first half of my first year. Yet, we've become great friends. And we both have dogs," he said.

And then he said, "Oh, by the way, I found a debate partner and we're considering going for the moot court contest."

"I thought that was a 2L deal."

"Normally, yes, but we're a great team, and it could be fun. There'll be sixteen other law schools in the competition."

Over the next several months, Chris prepared for one side of the case. Since each school can put forward more than one team, they had internal competition. Each case is assigned beforehand, so you know which side to study so you can prepare your oral arguments.

In our Friday meetings it was like watching a gifted young composer at work. Chris had a grasp of the black letter law and the underlying philosophical principles. I witnessed him grappling with what he called the "courtroom antics." He was training his neurons to say what he meant – and to develop a reserve of trained behaviors to summon up when the opposing counsel says something you didn't anticipate.

Our coffees moved to the Starbucks in his neighborhood. Sometimes we'd role play for 45 minutes or more, debating each other with relish. I found myself looking forward to Fridays for a completely new set of reasons!

When the weekend of the Moot Court came, they won their first-round debate. For the next round, the competition managers assigned them the opposite position. They had 45 minutes to prepare. They sequestered to organize who would speak first and what would be their newfound strategy and justifications.

We went for coffee (naturally) while he and his partner worked. They won again!

After that, they drew straws to learn which side they must argue. And, to my pride, they won again!

Seeing my son become animated through finding his courtroom voice enthralled me.

The Moot Court came down to the last round of Georgetown vs Fordham. Chris and his partner had submitted their written briefs on the case weeks earlier. Now they had argued on both sides of the case twice to reach the finals.

In the final, you go before three people who are real judges in their day job. They wear robes and sit on a dais. All the other teams (that you have defeated) and their coaches and families file into an auditorium that serves as the courtroom. The judges interrupt and disagree with you. They try to throw you off your cadence and train of thought.

Chris and his partner demurred several times instead of taking the judges' bait. It was an impressive battle between the teams and between each team and the judges. I could feel the drama in full flight.

Finally, the team from Fordham delivered what I heard as platitudes at the end of their closing arguments. They praised the American judicial process and the rule of law. I thought it was a bit over the top.

But the judges liked it and awarded them first prize. Chris's written brief won, too. Phew, what a roundhouse experience from law school coffees to animated Starbucks' role plays! Chris and his partner had triumphed in their first year of law school in the Moot Court competition.

In the spring, the river thawed and I began to row again. I treasured our talks over that first year of law school. At one point, Chris came to me with a tough decision to make. He had managed to balance working full time at DHS and attending class at night. But he wanted to graduate with his classmates by switching to the day program. This meant he had to quit DHS and take on debt to pay tuition and living expenses.

He shared his thought process with me, immediately letting me know that he was not asking me for a loan. He just wanted to brainstorm with me. It was like watching a student display their work on a complicated math problem. I was honored that he came to me for this kind of advice.

He knew I had spent years helping others make financial decisions in early-stage business. We weighed the options together. There were pros and cons to graduating with a substantial debt. However, he found a government loan program that would allow him to defer payments for up to ten years during the lower earning years of his law career. In the end, Chris decided to take on the debt necessary to graduate with his classmates in Section 3.

It is never too late to build the relationship you want: Ask for time…and maybe coffee.

Systematic Deposits into our Love Wellth Accounts

Our Friday meetings were punctuated by text messages between us. Sometimes, these went on in a stream-of-consciousness that could be better characterized as live conversations. The delightful difference with texting is that you get to consider what to say longer than in an actual conversation.

These texts are gone now. I wish I had sent them to email and printed and stored them. They were a precious lens into my son's life and our renewed relationship. But even with them gone, what remains is the indelible memory of our connection and the joy it brought both of us.

Love Wellth™ in Action

Love Wellth: Nurturing meaningful relationships requires dedicated time and effort, fostering stronger bonds and deeper connections. #lovewellth

Big Picture – Zoom Out

Love Wellth emphasizes the significance of nurturing relationships through consistent, dedicated interactions. It underscores that maintaining strong connections, especially with family, requires conscious effort and scheduled time for meaningful engagement. It highlights that even amidst busy schedules and life's demands, prioritizing quality time with loved ones can lead to stronger bonds and more fulfilling relationships.

Tactics – Ideas to Action

By implementing these tactics, you will strengthen bonds with loved ones and cultivate fulfilling relationships that enrich life's journey, and discover the power of **Love Wellth** for your life:

☐ **Schedule Dedicated Time:** Proactively schedule regular time for meaningful interactions with loved ones, even if it's just for 30 minutes.

☐ **Choose a Consistent Time and Place:** Establishing a routine, like a weekly coffee meeting, online chat or phone call can make it easier to prioritize and maintain consistency.

☐ **Engage in Empathetic Listening:** Actively listen and engage in conversations that allow for deeper understanding and connection.

☐ **Be Present and Attentive:** Minimize distractions during these scheduled interactions to demonstrate genuine interest and presence.

☐ **Embrace Various Communication Methods:** Utilize text messages or other forms of communication to maintain a continuous connection and share thoughts or experiences.

☐ **Don't Delay Reaching Out:** Take the initiative to connect with family and friends, remembering that "Someday" is not a day in the week.

Your Turn 🖎

Name one "8 AM Coffee" meeting that you need with someone in your life.

How can you make time to build/rebuild that relationship?

What might happen if you reach out today?

Name three ways you can heal a treasured relationship.

Chapter 7

Spirit Wellth

**"The moment I chose forgiveness, a
bluebird set off from my heart
to heal me."**

JC Chamberlain, Sr

Even amidst trauma and unexpected life challenges, there is an opportunity for profound personal growth and the discovery of inner strength. This chapter encourages readers to view challenging experiences as opportunities for resilience and spiritual connection. The accident led to a deep awareness of my **Spirit Wellth**, an understanding of myself, and a renewed appreciation for life.

The Split Second That Changed my Course

In the nearly fatal bicycle accident I mentioned earlier, the SUV driver was headed south on a country road, on-the-gas, accelerating through 50 mph. He had decided to jump the stop sign to beat a heavy truck that was coming east. Preoccupied with the truck, he didn't see Pete and me on our bikes until I was on the hood of his car.

It happened in a split second. By the time he took his foot off the gas, I had already been thrown 100 feet. I landed face down in gravel on the opposite side of the intersection.

It was a Saturday afternoon. Pete and I were cycling east to meet a group of our teammates coming west. As it turns out, we never would have met up with them, because we were on the wrong road – at the wrong time.

Pete and I were working well together, taking turns in the lead, rolling around 25 miles per hour. That is what racers do. I just happened to be in the lead when the SUV came from our left and knocked me out. Just four feet behind, Pete missed being hit, but, poor guy, he saw everything.

If you hold a cup of water to your lips, it takes about a half second to take a sip. That's how long it took for my body to collide with the large vehicle. Take a moment to imagine the impact unfolding in slow motion...

My front wheel hit the right fender of the SUV.

My left knee took the first impact, turning me from going east to heading south.

As the car raced on, I carved a trough in the sheet metal with my knee, two-feet long and two-inches deep, over the front tire.

My rib cage tore off the right rear-view mirror from back to front as I whiplashed down the car.

My helmet smacked the car's steel frame above the front passenger window.

My elbow broke through the rear passenger window, putting my left shoulder inside the car.

The window frame crushed my shoulder, separated me from my bike, and the momentum of the car threw me 100 feet across the intersection.

Two people had a front row seat to the impact and saw me being thrown from my bike in that instant. Later, they each said they assumed I was dead. By chance, both were medical professionals. The driver was a professor of emergency medicine and my buddy Pete was the head of anesthesiology at his hospital.

As they ran up to my lifeless body, their medical training kicked in. They checked and found I had a pulse and was breathing and they realized I was just knocked out. I was *really* out, but alive. I have been told these details, as I have no recollection of being hit. Funny how the mind works.

But the body keeps score.

In the ambulance, I was vaguely aware of a siren. I mentioned it to Pete who had jumped in with me. I was floating in and out of consciousness and probably in shock. Pete asked me who to call. I remembered my (future wife and) girlfriend Jill's phone number before I checked out again.

The Miracles Begin

At one moment, I left my body and found myself in the presence of the Higher Power. I felt unafraid and welcome to ask about anything. Without needing to speak, I asked:

- "Why me?"
- "Why this?"
- "Why now?"
- "Why here?"
- "What do you want from me?"

God's response came instantly to me *as though we were one spirit* and could simply converse this way. God told me:

"There was a fatal accident one day in your future that only I can see. Because I am not done with you, I chose this accident because it is survivable. That is your choice. And if you do, it will change the course of your life so that the fatal accident is no longer in your future."

That was it.

90 minutes later, I awoke looking up at a person wearing a mask and surgical gown. She was pulling a string out of my forehead. She cut the string. She poked something into my chin a few times. And then cut a string again. Stitches?

"Uh oh," I thought. "Why would I need stitches?"

When she walked away, I could see Jill on my right. Then I realized I couldn't turn my head.

"Where am I?" I asked

"You were in a bad accident on your bicycle," she said. "You're in a hospital. You're safe here."

I tried to sit up and realized that my neck was braced. I couldn't move anything except my eyes! Terrified at my immobility, I glanced at Jill.

"Is my bike okay?"

I asked without thinking twice about anything else. Should I have wondered if I was going to survive this? Would I be able to walk? Will I be able to ride?

Pete was standing near the foot of my bed in street clothes. This seemed strange, but things were starting to sink in. I thought we were riding, but now we're in a hospital, and I need stitches. And one more thing.

A stranger was holding my left hand. I tried to hold his hand in return, but couldn't. I stared up in wonder at my awkward inability to squeeze his hand. His eyes were big with a look of surprise mixed with relief. We just stared at each other. I didn't know that this was the driver of the SUV that hit me, standing there, holding my hand.

I had no idea that I was covered in blood, with tubes and wires threaded around the neck brace. My mouth felt swollen, and I could taste blood behind my teeth. My mouth was parched.

"Can I have some water?"

Jill said softly, "No, John, you'll probably go into surgery, but first they're going to take you for x-rays."

"Surgery? Why?"

I closed my eyes and drifted off.

Trauma 4

When I woke up, I was in a room on what seemed to be an upper floor. I could see the top of the building out the window. It was still a sunny day! Ironically, I remember thinking: "Too bad I can't move, because it's a beautiful day to go on a bike ride!"

Jill sat quietly reading a book across the room.

"Where are we?" I asked.

"This is Trauma 4, a room they put you in until you're stable enough for surgery. They need to take an MRI to assess the extent of your injuries."

A staff person came into the room. He wheeled my bed *with* the IV pole out into the hallway. Alone in the elevator, I got a chill as we descended to the "B" level where another person in scrubs met us. Neither of these men seemed to understand that I was in extraordinary pain. They picked me up on the bed sheet and swung me from the hospital bed to the ice-cold MRI platen like I was a wet rug. The narrow platen didn't support my shoulders, so it pushed directly on my spine.

The cavernous hospital basement seemed to have 40-foot ceilings. The massive MRI machine towered over me. It was terrifying, like being in a dungeon in a medieval torture chamber.

One of the technicians handed me what he called a "kill switch." He said, "Push the button if the pain is too much or if you just can't continue. Some people feel claustrophobic inside the MRI, and the test takes a while."

Over the next 15 minutes, I hit the "kill switch" three times. The icey platen would slowly slide back out of the machine. The roaring sound of the machine combined with the cold and the extraordinary pain really freaked me out. They finally gave up and took me back to Jill in Trauma 4.

Soon, they rolled in a sit-up X-Ray machine. They raised the back of the bed, then leaned me forward to place an X-Ray film behind me. Another ice-cold, rock-hard plate on my spine! Finally they lowered the bed so I could rest.

We waited. I couldn't move anything except the fingers on my right hand.

A man came in wearing a surgical outfit with booties and an optical scope flipped up above his glasses. He pulled down his mask and put his hand on my good hand.

"Mr. Chamberlain, I'm an orthopedic trauma surgeon. Your left shoulder is broken in three places, but it's not bad enough to need surgery."

In my sales and management career, I have spent 45 years reading people's body language for a living. He said it was good news, but his lack of eye contact told me he was actually disappointed. By contrast, I was incredibly happy to hear this because I was 57 and had never had surgery of any kind. I even still had my tonsils.

He left and I slumped back into the bed. Jill moved a chair closer and held my good hand. I could feel tears rolling down my cheeks. She reached up and brushed them away and said something very reassuring that I will never forget:

"John, we will get through this together."

She just seemed to know. This made all the difference at a time when nothing seemed for sure.

The Good News and the Bad News

Later on, a kind-looking man in a lab coat came in. At first he made good eye contact, and I felt a bit relieved that he was going to shoot the news to me straight.

"Sir, you have six fractures in your spine, and three more in your pubic bone. Each of these will heal in time. It may take many months," he warned, "but we should not risk spine surgery for these kinds of fractures." He was looking at the floor while he said the last part about not risking surgery.

He then said, "With hard work, you should be able to learn to walk again. But you probably will *not* be able to ride a bicycle."

I was so dumbfounded by his prediction that I was initially at a loss for words. Then I found my voice.

"Sir, you don't know who you're saying that to. I'm not sure how I will do it, but I *will* walk, and I *will* learn to ride again." Through my tears, I added, with as much emphasis as I could muster, "I cannot imagine a life without walking and riding."

He looked at me like I was delusional and moved to leave.

With my tongue, I could feel the hole between two of my front teeth every time I spoke. I grimaced and asked if I would be seeing a dental surgeon.

He answered, "Oh, no, we don't do dental work here. You take care!" And with that, he walked out.

When visiting hours ended, a reluctant Jill had to go home.

I'd felt drained by the last doctor's curt bedside manner and drifted in and out as the morphine kicked in.

I awoke to a voice calling my name.

"John?"

"Is that you?" the voice asked.

In the darkened room, and without my glasses, I could make out the outline of a tall figure with white hair. After my out-of-body conversation with God earlier in the day, I quickly concluded it was now time for the *in*-person interview.

As my eyes adjusted, I realized it wasn't God after all, but my dear friend and fellow cyclist Ralph Antolino. I was so relieved to see him, especially, since I assumed I was now off the hook for passing into heaven or going to hell.

My Mother Arrives!

Mom arrived from Dayton and commanded the staff to bring a bed into my room for her. They did. She stayed next to me until the morning of my discharge. *(More on that day soon.)*

Later that morning, my phone rang. The screen had been cracked in the crash, but it worked! Mom pressed the talk button and held the phone on speaker so we could both listen. It was my scout troop Committee Chairman, Claude.

Without any preamble, he said, with a deep sigh, "JC, I have terrible news."

He told me that one of my Eagle Scouts, Mark, had been murdered with a butcher knife the previous night, by some boy Mark knew, in what appeared to be a fit of insanity.

I was so astonished to hear this that I could not speak! My heart was so heavy – my eyes darted around the top of the room, looking for something, some way to hold back tears. They welled up anyway and began to roll down my cheeks.

"Hello?" he asked into the empty line.

"I'm here, Claude, but I don't have words."

"Yeah, I get it. The family is distraught, as you can well imagine."

I finally mustered the words to say, "I am so sorry. What can I do?"

"The family wants you to speak at the memorial service this Saturday."

"Claude, you know I would do that in a heartbeat – if I could."

I let that sink in for a moment as I confronted, for the very first time, the delicate matter of separating the trauma of the crash from any description of the crash.

"I was in a bad accident yesterday, Claude, and I'm in a hospital in Columbus, Ohio."

"So sorry, JC! I had no idea! What happened?"

"I am not even sure yet, but I'm only able to move my right hand. My mom is here holding the phone for me." Thinking quickly, I asked, "If I write something, will you read it for me? Will you stand in for me at the service?" He agreed.

We signed off and I slumped back into the mattress, sobbing uncontrollably. Mom held my good hand as she wept, too. She loved my scouts like they were her own kids. She'd been the den mother when I was in Cub Scouts. All these emotions came rushing back in the moment.

I felt defeated.

As Monday arrived, I realized I had better let my boss, Bruce, know that I wouldn't be coming in – for a long while. Mom dialed and held the phone. After telling him what happened, he said, without hesitation:

"You tell me your bank account numbers, and I'll deposit your checks until you're back. Don't spend a minute worrying about us. You heal up, JC."

I hung up and closed my eyes in prayer. What a blessing to have a boss who would say that without seeming to think twice! Somewhere, I must have paid it forward to deserve this.

I also called Wyc, my friend who was organizing our Alumni Eight group for the Head of the Charles Regatta in Boston the next Saturday. I told him what had happened. For only the second time in 30 years, we were getting our undefeated college rowing team together in the Grand Masters category. Alas, I now realized that our "dream" row next weekend would not include me.

Then it hit me that I would have been forced to choose between rowing and speaking at my Eagle Scout's memorial. Of course, I would have chosen the memorial service.

God has a wonderful way of restructuring our lives to simplify our choices to do only what matters most.

I wished Wyc the absolute best of luck in the Head of the Charles Regatta, and soon drifted off again, in pain, and sad to my core about losing my Eagle Scout, Mark.

Painful Progress

The next day was marked by an invasion of three hospital staff who came into my room, armed with huge straps and – in my opinion – not much charm. They sat me up – making me wince – strapped the belts around my ungracefully open-back gown and lifted me to my feet. Simultaneously, they proclaimed I would walk on my own to the bathroom (eight feet away) by Friday. It was hard to imagine.

My left knee, the first point of impact with the SUV, had swollen to the size of a grapefruit. A week later, another X-Ray revealed that a chip of bone attached to my MCL (behind the kneecap) had separated from its proper location. Since the hospital apparently "did not do" this sort of work either, I found an orthopedic sports specialist who took three turkey-baster-sized syringes of blood out of my knee. He then fit me with a Neoprene and Velcro "cast" that immobilized my knee for the next two months.

I could see already that to get through this I had to take charge of my own healthcare decisions. Simultaneously, I did feel woefully unprepared to advocate for my needs. The staff plied me with morphine every four hours, which clouded my mental clarity, albeit with the added benefit of taking the edge off my aching pain.

Luckily, I had Mom.

She defended me. And she held my feet, which had a grounding effect for me. That meant so much. Since each trauma surgeon left without scheduling surgery, now the collective goal of staff seemed to be to get me walking enough to send me home.

When You Tell Me I Can't Do Something...

A Physical Therapy team of four came in, belted me up, and got me to the bathroom door. An investment in my future, I guessed, because I was still peeing in the urinal cup so they could track if my kidneys were working. Beyond the simplicity of my 13 fractures, there was a massive amount of soft tissue damage. Plus, they were still concerned about organ damage.

All good so far. It was amazing that I took off a rearview mirror with my ribcage at 55 miles per hour, wearing only a cycling jersey, and didn't break a rib. But, boy, was I bruised!

Working together, Mom interviewed me about my experiences with Eagle Scout Mark. We completed his eulogy in between visits of physical and neurological experts. As each new team arrived, Mom would let them know directly that she was my guardian, there to protect me in my drugged and damaged state.

Mom encouraged me and helped me make the calls to a few friends whom I thought should know what had happened. She was a deeply faithful Christian who believed that it would help my healing if I could expand prayer circles in my church and cycling communities.

A brain injury specialist came in and ran me through logic puzzles and a long series of very tricky questions with dependent variables. It was actually fun, and I was grateful to have my mental faculties, which seemed to be intact.

Later that day, and with emotional difficulty, I finished the eulogy for Mark. Mom transcribed it and emailed it to Claude, who printed and displayed it at the service. 16 Eagle Scouts from our troop walked in lock-step with the family on their day of mourning. It made me proud that they showed such compassion and the will to drop whatever they were doing to show up for the family and their fallen friend. The largest church in town was standing-room-only for the service. My Assistant Scoutmaster read the eulogy. Mark's father stood and spoke in unwavering love for his son.

So many showed extraordinary strength that day.

Ralph told me that a friend of his had just become the president of this hospital after leading a turnaround at another one with the same ownership. I asked my Primary Care

Manager (PCM) if I could meet with this man, as we had a mutual acquaintance. He was "not available this week," they told me.

So I didn't get to share with the new president of the hospital my opinion of my treatment, for example. But I noticed an increase in the attention I received, and the staff's attitude seemed to change for the better. Apparently, I knew someone who was important to them.

I could hear in the voice of my PCM an urgency to get me out of there. I began to feel like a liability.

I asked her, "How is it that I've been here five days with obvious oral trauma, and I've been seen by specialists for every other part of my body except my teeth?"

Her response was astonishing to me. "Mr. Chamberlain, dental is not an emergency or trauma function in this hospital. We haven't hired dental trauma specialists for many years. You'll need to schedule that specialty when you're discharged."

And so it went. I asked pesky questions and Mom defended me as my advocate. She called my friend Drake and he referred me to a dentist who supports the Columbus Blue Jackets pro hockey team. *They* have dental trauma – almost every game!

Then, PT came in without their belts. I made it to the door and down the hallway to the elevator doors, with Jill pushing the IV pole and me holding her arm. They had succeeded in getting me ready to go home – as advertised. I was still peeing in a cup and had not had a shower nor a "sponge bath" since my arrival nearly a week ago following a 62-mile bike ride.

Mom Goes Home

Mom, who had been there for the critical few days when I could barely manage for myself, left for Dayton, assuming that Jill would be visiting me over the weekend. Suddenly, a new

Primary Care Manager appeared whom I had not seen before. With barely a greeting, she coarsely announced "You have to leave today or pay for tomorrow out of your own pocket. Your insurance has run out."

"What?!?" I said. I had no evidence of this. And I had not been warned of such an imminent situation by the weekday staff. What could possibly have happened?

Perhaps I should go home! But where would I go? I live in Virginia! How would I get there? I had no glasses. My car was parked 25 miles away. I could barely walk, let alone drive! My Mom, my defender, left this morning.

I hastily called Jill, who had been planning to visit later. She had no idea that Mom had returned to Dayton and she hadn't been informed that I would be discharged – today. We carefully installed me in her car, using pillows and blankets. Even on morphine, I still winced with every movement. My soft tissue damage was significant, and my fractured pubic bone seemed to be involved in every motion.

It did not occur to me that I should have received written discharge orders by the attending physician referring me to a long-term rehabilitation hospital. And in the sudden fear that somehow my insurance had "run out," I acquiesced to being discharged on the weekend by this new supposed Primary Care Manager.

This was all very upsetting.

As it turned out, my insurance had *not* run out; the PCM had misread my case, and I could have stayed longer!

Healing and Miracles

Thank God for Jill, who came to my rescue. For four days, I slept on a cot in her living room, still unable to shower since the accident. I learned then that I had to have my doctor sign a document to prove that I was not MI/MR (mentally impaired/mentally retarded) in order to be admitted to a rehabilitation hospital.

I had no local doctor since I didn't live in that state. And the hospital wouldn't agree to process the form – because I was no longer an inpatient. This was so aggravating to me in my helpless state of pain and immobility! I had to navigate this new challenge without a local doctor, on my own ingenuity, from a wooden chair in my girlfriend's dining room.

In the end, I called a friend who was the Director of the Ohio Department of Health. He later told me that the people asking for the MI/MR proof sheet did not report to him. But, magically, a few hours after I called him, the requirement was waived, clearing my path to admission into long term care.

For me, it was a miracle.

Once I arrived at the rehab hospital, I made painstaking progress through my determination to regain strength. Many of the early flexibility and strength exercises ended in tears. The staff would wheel me back to my room and transfer me back into my bed, where I spent the rest of the day. I challenged my brain with timed puzzles. They began to teach me how to walk again, how to maneuver my injuries to use a washing machine and how to cook for myself.

It amazed me how much we take for granted the simplest things we do each day!

As I progressed, other patients noticed.

One had become so obese she could not walk. My nurse came to my room one day and asked if I would be willing to talk with the woman. I consented and she wheeled me into the woman's room. The bedridden woman told me how much she admired my determination and progress.

It was an honor to encourage her as I told her I had confidence in her ability to walk again. And then we prayed together. She thanked me and invited me to give witness at her church if she ever got to go home.

Six weeks later, she was able to walk enough to do exactly that!

Meanwhile, I brought my champion's attitude to each thing I was asked to do. I treated my breathing exercises like sport. And I took four teaspoons of Omega 3 fish oil twice every day. Research I had read said that fish oil could lower inflammation, and that inflammation is the root cause of most diseases.

Looking back, I find it more important that I *believed* the research than any science the article said backed up their claims. Belief is a powerful element of the human psyche, as shown by the Reiki energy work I did remotely twice every day with two different masters.

Reiki was an unfamiliar practice for me. It was proposed by my mother and my father who each said they had benefited from working with masters they knew in different parts of the country. My experience during the Reiki sessions developed into feeling a very intimate connection with the loving energy I believe surrounds the earth. I got so I could "see down a pipe" to the masters through this energy during our 20-minute sessions, giving me a strong sense of connection with each of them that enhanced my ability to benefit from this invisible energy therapy.

I looked forward to these guided sessions over the seven weeks I lived in the rehabilitation hospital; they helped me *feel* myself healing. It was a very calm sensation that resulted from engaging with a loving energy source.

And I felt the love.

My church sent 35 get well cards and a prayer quilt. I felt an outpouring of love from my communities. A cycling friend put my name into a prayer chain that circulated within the Jewish community. My work gave me all the flexibility to focus on healing by putting my paychecks directly into my bank account. Like my mom, Jill had been an invaluable solace to me.

Then I felt the miracle.

30 days after the accident, I went to see my neurologist and they did a scan of the six fractures in my spine.

To my amazement and joy, he told me, "You have the spine of a normal 50-year-old. I don't need to see you again."

I was incredulous. I wanted to see what he saw, so he invited me to view the 360-degree scan at the workstation computer. It was fascinating. He pointed to the vertebra in my spine, which had been fractured by the impact with the SUV. We looked at the "before," and then we looked at the "30-day scan."

Each fracture was healed.

"You're ready to go home, John. Just keep doing what you're doing."

I praised God for the interventions, the caring and the healing I experienced.

How I Healed

I feel that the love I received through caring medical and non-medical professionals, the numerous prayers and prayer quilt, the Reiki, the supplements, and my positive attitude toward physical therapy played key roles in my healing.

My life was spared for some unknown reason and the time had come to get back to that life to find out the blessings and adventures of my future.

Perhaps feeling that I was on this path for a reason had something to do with my resolve to give healing the best chance. Two months after the accident, I was cleared to get on an indoor spinning bike. Three months later, my friend and business partner, Christophe, put me on the back of a tandem bicycle and we began to ride everyday. At first it was five miles, then 10, then further.

We became known as the "odd couple" by some cyclists who made fun of us on the tandem and what was obviously our close relationship. These people had no idea what I had been through.

We rode 5,000 miles that year on the tandem. By the end of the year, I had regained enough confidence and muscle tone to try a single bike. I realized then, 14 months after the accident, that I could balance on my own again.

What an extraordinary gift Christophe gave me!

My faith and determination had carried me through the worst days after the accident.

And love and community lifted me the rest of the way.

Back Home

My future stepson Brian generously drove me back to Virginia. On the drive, I laid on a bed of eggshell foam and blankets in the front seat of my car. The very next day I went to the home of the slain scout's family. I had not called ahead; I knew I should just go. I remember getting there on my own, managing to drive with a cast on my left leg and crutches on the seat beside me.

I rang the doorbell and, as I waited, I tried to fight back the tears that were coming, to no avail. Mark's parents and I cried together as we remembered Mark so fondly. It felt important to grieve and carry on. Mark loved the Model UN debates, and taught English in South Korea before enrolling at the Georgetown University Law Center. Somehow, we were able to laugh about the good times we had all shared with this remarkable young man.

It was as though we could only fill with joy what had suddenly been deeply carved with sorrow.

Healing and...Forgiveness

I'd worked on healing – and then I needed to work on forgiveness. After all, I'd had an inspiring conversation with God about *why* I was in this accident. I'd felt Him telling me that my time had not come. I was needed here; there was work to do.

That amazing moment with God helped me process His forgiveness through my own personal humanness and humanity.

Once I understood who the man was who had hit me and then followed the ambulance to the hospital, where he tenderly held my hand, it changed my impression of him. Yes, it had been his fault and I had expenses to pay. And I had to heal. But I began to think about how far reparations needed to go.

I had a great personal injury lawyer. After returning home, I made numerous trips back to Ohio to work through legal details with him. It was during one of those meetings that he announced, "We can go after the million dollar 401k of the driver who hit you. It will take a couple of years and many depositions, but it could be successful and lucrative."

At that moment, I was struck with the realization that resounded through my whole being: I wanted to forgive this man and I did not want to ruin his life.

Already, and with deep clarity, I knew I would find a way to survive and heal. I also didn't want to ruin *my* life over this. As I chose forgiveness, I felt a Bluebird light off from my heart to heal me. And I was submerged in a profound sense of relief.

When my focus returned to the room and my lawyer, I told him that I had decided to drop it. To my relief, he exclaimed, "John, that's the best news I've heard all year!"

That forgiveness was another split-second that changed my course.

As to the unhinged kid who stabbed my scout, there was no consolation for Mark's family or our scout community. Aside from the years it took to prosecute him for murder, we had to collectively let go of a loss we could not change. My time with Mark's family remembering him helped a deep wound heal in my heart. It seemed impossible to fathom such a crime. But we had to find a path forward through our love of each other, in the bosom of our small community.

Eventually, I had to examine all the anger that remained with me toward the hospital: the insensitivity to my pain during the MRI, the less than sympathetic interactions with the staff, the lack of caring for my broken teeth, the abrupt and improper discharge from the hospital – all of it was difficult for me to reconcile.

Ultimately, I decided to pierce my armor of anger with the most transforming spiritual tenet I knew: gratitude. The hospital and its staff provided the urgent care and medical analysis I needed to survive. I chose to be grateful for the care I did receive.

More Miracles

Mom had gone home. She went to her favorite local grocery store, the Dorothy Lane Market, where she ran into a Jewish friend she had not seen for six months.

"Hi Jane! How are you? What have you been up to?" her friend asked.

"I just returned from Columbus where my son was hit by a car and is in the trauma ward."

"Really?" she said. "What's his name?"

"John Chamberlain. Why do you ask?"

"Because I just came from Synagogue, and we prayed for someone named John Chamberlain, a cyclist, who had been hit by a car and needed our prayers."

They stood looking at each other – incredulous. Tears of joy flowed and they embraced.

As it turns out, my dear friend and a professional triathlete in Atlanta, Mike, had learned about my accident through the grapevine of our shared cycling community. He had put my name into a nationwide prayer chain that circulates throughout the Jewish community.

Since my Mom goes by her birth name of Jane Mayo, her Jewish friend did not connect praying for me with her friend Jane!

Interfaith healing prayers coming to me from all over the country! Powerful!

Universal, spiritual, healing strength coming from on high! Wonderful!

The body is in the Spirit! Hallelujah!

Spirit Wellth™ in Action

Even amidst trauma and unexpected life challenges, there is an opportunity for profound personal growth and the discovery of inner strength. This chapter encourages readers to view challenging experiences as opportunities for resilience and spiritual connection, leading to a deeper understanding of oneself and a renewed appreciation for life. #spiritwellth

Big Picture – Zoom Out

Can you view seemingly insurmountable challenges as opportunities for spiritual growth and self-discovery? I have shared a near-fatal cycling accident and the subsequent physical and emotional recovery process. Through this experience, I found solace and strength in unexpected places, particularly through a deep connection with a higher power, unwavering support from loved ones, and a resilient mindset that refused to accept limitations. Spirit Wellth inspires individuals to tap into their inner strength and resilience when facing adversity, finding meaning and purpose even in the darkest moments. It underscores that our spirit, much like our physical bodies, can heal and grow stronger through adversity.

Tactics – Ideas to Action

Cultivate a Mindset of Resilience:

☐ Embrace challenges as opportunities for growth and learning, even when they are painful or unexpected.

☐ Challenge limiting beliefs and predictions, choosing instead to focus on your inner strength and potential for healing.

☐ Draw inspiration from my determination to walk and ride again, despite medical professionals suggesting otherwise.

Seek Support and Connection:

☐ Lean on your support system during challenging times, accepting help and comfort from those who offer it.

☐ Recognize the power of community, prayer, and shared experiences in navigating difficult emotions and finding strength.

☐ Engage in acts of kindness and support for others, even while in the midst of personal hardship, recognizing the reciprocal nature of caring and connection.

Engage in Self-Advocacy:

☐ When facing medical challenges or unexpected situations, actively participate in your care plan and ask questions.

☐ Don't be afraid to seek second opinions or advocate for your needs, particularly when experiencing discomfort or uncertainty.

☐ Use your network and resources to connect with professionals who can address your specific needs.

Embrace Spirituality:

- ☐ Explore your personal connection to spirituality, whether through faith, meditation, or connection with nature.

- ☐ Find solace and guidance in your chosen spiritual practice, particularly during times of uncertainty or emotional distress.

- ☐ Recognize the potential for spiritual experiences to bring comfort, meaning, and a sense of peace during challenging times.

Find Strength in Shared Experiences:

- ☐ Share your story with others who have experienced similar challenges, finding solace and understanding in shared experiences.

- ☐ Offer support to others who are going through difficult times, drawing on your own resilience and lessons learned.

- ☐ Recognize the transformative power of storytelling and shared experiences in building connection and fostering empathy.

Your Turn ✍

Has someone you know been through a traumatic accident?

Were they content with (or would change) their healthcare self-advocacy?

Reflect on the role of being an advocate for yourself or someone.

How could your caregivers have responded differently?

Were they sensitive to your emotional health as well as your physical health?

If not, how can you work on forgiving them?

Conclusion

Conclusion: $1+1 = 11$

Discover that you already have a positive balance in your **Emotional Bank Accounts**. Within the **EMOTIONAL WELLTH FRAMEWORK**, you can create the best chance for an optimal outcome in your life.

These stories helped me to share a new beginning in my life after a terrible setback. I consider the impact with the car as a wake-up to these realizations. I'm so glad that I was the first one through the intersection that fateful day. I'm grateful to be able to share my sometimes-difficult journey and the transcendent joy of newfound resilience.

I have come to the conclusion that life is sufficiently unpredictable so as to be worth living. My setback became a path to understanding that I had made years of deposits into my **Emotional Wellth** accounts. These deep resources flowed from my life of social engagement, exercise and caring for others. My friends, family, and co-workers believed in me the way I had believed in them over many years.

My journey and these stories revealed what I call **Emotional Wellth**. As I peered through layers of negative thoughts, behaviors and habits, I saw myself falling down an Arc of Loneliness. My first timid steps to climbing out of my paralysis were facilitated by those who believed in me.

The lens of a new **Emotional Wellth Framework** enabled me to receive their caring, to re-engage with them in new and meaningful ways. The few dark years after the crash sat in contrast to my lifelong learning, earning, giving, and loving.

My glass was not empty, it was overflowing! I witnessed these supportive resources raising me from a descent into loneliness to float up on a rising tide in which 1+1=11.

Emotional Wellth Framework™

Prostate Cancer Presents a New Test

Five years after the car crash, I received a diagnosis of advanced stage prostate cancer. On a 1-to-4 scale, I had 3b cancer, with a 9 out of 10 Gleason Score (which predicts the growth and spread of the cancer). The numbers said my cancer was both dense and aggressive.

A normal prostate is 12 grams. They took *90 grams* of tumor from me in a six-hour Davinci robot-assisted surgery. Because it was so pervasive, they said I would need antiandrogen chemotherapy for the rest of my life.

Bad news, right?

I prepared for my surgery thinking about all I had discovered after the car vs. bike accident with positive mental phrasing. I praised "God in me," looked to the resources I would bring to endure the substantial operation and months of recovery. Armed with my amazing community and deep well of fitness, I activated my **Emotional Wellth** network.

I shared the diagnosis, surgery and recovery process with each person who had played a role in my car crash healing. I created an acronym to bring awareness to the Prostate Specific Antigen (PSA) test, which is how men discover whether they have prostate cancer or not.

"P" is for Preparation and Prevention

"S" is for Symptoms and Surgery

"A" is for Awareness and Analysis

I accepted invitations to speak publicly about this disease that kills 20,000 men in the U.S. every year. Using the PSA acronym as my outline, I scripted a three-minute public service announcement to raise awareness and demystify the disease (a PSA for PSA!).

With Preparation and Prevention, we can identify Symptoms, and Schedule Surgery (if needed). By being Aware and using Analysis, we can stay ahead of this common, deadly form of cancer.

The chemo they prescribed for me is called "Lupron," a brand of leuprolide that effectively turns off the pituitary. Lupron stops the body from making testosterone, which is what prostate cancer uses to grow. There's a long list of side effects including depression, weight gain and osteoporosis from the dosage set by pharmacologists.

From the outset, my mind-set was: "The drug company doesn't know me!"

Every six months, I would get a bolus from a huge needle in my butt cheek.

"Oh, man!" I thought, "We're right back to my fear of needles that began when I had to get bicillin as a four year old. Except now I have the perspective of newfound resilience in my **Emotional Wellth Framework.**"

At my lowest ebb, I was depressed and experiencing weight gain, well-known side effects of Lupron. One day, I was at Green Lizard Cycling, my favorite bike store in Virginia. The owner Beth noticed I was out of sorts. In what became a turning point in my recovery, she offered that I could use their indoor training lab to get my cycling back on track. It consisted of 16 stations located at the back of the store. As you know from the chapter on Learning Wellth, I hate spinning bikes. But this was different. I used my own bike on an indoor resistance trainer. So I could coast when I needed to and the terrain was more like outdoor riding. After trying it reluctantly I returned again and again. Over the next 5 years I rode 525 90-minute sessions. I climbed out of my despair, reconnected with my fellow cyclists and found a new kind of balance using an indoor trainer.

I continued to ride about 7,500 miles a year. And I would start to feel better before the end of each six-month shot cycle. Then something interesting happened. We missed a shot by 90 days during the pandemic because of supply-chain disruptions.

Surprise! Shock! Gratitude! My PSA stayed at *zero*, even with the delayed shot. At my quarterly appointment with my urologist, I asked if they'd modify my dose, considering the zero score and my level of physical activity. His answer: "No."

"I want to go off Lupron, Doc."

He reminded me of the severity of my case, extent of the surgery, and prognosis of a relapse if I quit using Lupron to control testosterone. We had a spirited discussion.

"Okay, so what's your tolerance for an increasing PSA?" he challenged me. "Is it a score of 5? Or 10?"

"My expectation is that my PSA will continue to be *zero*," I said simply.

He hesitated. Then he surprised me. "Game on, JC. You've exceeded expectations at every turn of your recovery. So, we'll skip this shot and I'll see you in 90 days."

He believed in me! Now, in 2024, it's three years later and my PSA is still *zero*. I'm intensely grateful.

And I rode my bike 10,000 miles last year.

I think back on that day in Dayton when Mom returned from my bedside in Trauma 4 in Columbus. She had run into her Jewish friend, whom she had not seen for six months, only to discover that her friend had just come from praying for me with others at her synagogue. Me, a complete stranger to them! Timing like that is never a coincidence – it's a spiritual appointment.

My **Emotional Wellth Framework** was already in place. Interfaith healing prayers, powerful prayers, were coming to me from all over the country! Once again I could feel a universal, spiritual, healing strength coming from on high.

Perhaps, the body is in the spirit instead of the other way around.

Consider this: We are spiritual beings having a human experience. And that can make all the difference.

Enjoy the ride!

JC Chamberlain, Sr

Made in the USA
Columbia, SC
15 December 2024

49473275R00090